Piero Coda

"THE CHURCH IS THE GOSPEL"

At the sources of Pope Francis' theology

LIBERIA EDITRICE VATICANA

Published in Australia by

© Copyright 2019 Coventry Press

Coventry Press
33 Scoresby Road
Bayswater Vic. 3153
Australia

Translated into English by Salesians of Don Bosco of the Province of Mary Help of Christians of Australia and The Pacific

ISBN 9780648497721

© Copyright 2017 - Libreria Editrice Vaticana
00120 Città del Vaticano
Tel. 06.698.81032 - Fax 06.698.84716
commerciale.lev@spc.va

All rights reserved. Other than for the purposes and subject to the conditions prescribed under the *Copyright Act*, no part of this publication may be reproduced, stored in a retrieval system, or transmitted in any form or by any means, electronic, mechanical, photocopying, recording or otherwise, without the prior permission of the publisher.

Cataloguing-in-Publication entry is available from the National Library of Australia http:/catalogue.nla.gov.au/.

Printed in Australia

www.coventrypress.com.au

SERIES
THE THEOLOGY OF POPE FRANCIS

JURGEN WERBICK: *God's Weakness for Humankind.* Pope Francis' view of God

LUCIO CASULA: *Faces, Gestures and Places.* Pope Francis' Christology

PETER HÜNERMANN: *Human Beings According to Christ Today.* Pope Francis' Anthropology

ROBERTO REPOLE: *The Dream of a Gospel-inspired Church.* Pope Francis' Ecclesiology

CARLOS GALLI: *Christ, Mary, the Church and the Peoples.* Pope Francis' Mariology

SANTIAGO MADRIGAL TERRAZAS: *'Unity Prevails over Conflict'.* Pope Francis' Ecumenism

ARISTIDE FUMAGALLI: *Journeying in Love.* Pope Francis' Moral Theology

JUAN CARLOS SCANNONE: *The Gospel of Mercy in the Spirit of Discernment.* Pope Francis' Social Ethics

MARINELLA PERRONI: *Kerygma and Prophecy.* Pope Francis' Biblical Hermeneutics

PIERO CODA: *'The Church is the Gospel'.* At the sources of Pope Francis' theology

MARKO IVAN RUPNIK: *According to the Spirit.* Spiritual theology on the move with Pope Francis' Church

ABBREVIATIONS

AL	*Amoris Laetitia*
DM	*Dives in Misericordia*
EG	*Evangelii Gaudium*
EN	*Evangelii Nuntiandi*
GD	*Gaudete in Domino*
GS	*Gaudium et Spes*
LG	*Lumen Gentium*
LS	*Laudato Si'*
MV	*Misericordiae Vultus*
OT	*Optatam Totius*
PP	*Populorum Progressio*
SE	*Spiritual Exercises*

PREFACE TO THE SERIES

From the time of his first appearance in St Peter's Square on the evening of his election, it was more than clear that Francis' pontificate would be adopting a new style. His modest apparel, calling himself the Bishop of Rome, asking the people to pray for him – in the 'deafening silence' of a packed square – and greeting them with a simple '*buonasera*' (good evening) ... these were all eloquent signs of the fact that there was a change taking place in the way the Pope related to people, and thus in the 'language' used.

The gestures and words that have followed from that occasion only confirm and strengthen this first impression. Indeed, it could be said that over the ensuing years, the image of the papacy has been decidedly transformed, involving a change that affects homilies, addresses and documents promulgated as well.

As could be predicted, this has generated divergent opinions, especially regarding his teaching. While many have in fact welcomed his magisterium with enthusiasm and deep interest, sensing the fresh wind of the gospel, some others have approached it in a more detached way and, at times, with suspicion. There has been no lack of more absolute views, even going as far as to doubt the existence of a theology in Francis' teaching.

A summary judgement of this kind could come from the very different backgrounds of Francis and his predecessor, Benedict XVI. The latter, we know, has been one of the most outstanding and important theologians of the twentieth century and undoubtedly relied on his personal theological development in his rich papal magisterium. We have not yet fully appreciated, nor will we cease to appreciate, the depth of this magisterium. What Bergoglio has behind him, on the other hand, is his long and deep-rooted experience as a religious and a pastor.

However, this does not mean that his magisterium is without a theology. The fact that he was not mostly, or only, a 'professional' theologian does not mean that his magisterium is not supported by a theology. Were this the case, we could say that, strictly speaking, the majority of his predecessors were without a theology, given that Ratzinger represents the exception rather than the rule.

In any case, the fact that we can discuss the theological significance of Francis' magisterium, as well as the fact that, very often, some of his highly evocative and very immediate expressions have been so abused as to rob them of their profundity – in the journalistic as well as the ecclesial ambit – makes the response of this series, which I have the honour of presenting, a significant one.

By drawing on the competence and rigorous study of theologians of proven worth, coming from diverse contexts, the series has sought to research the theological thinking which supports the Pope's teaching. It explores its roots, its freshness, and its continuity with earlier magisterium.

The result can be found in the eleven volumes which make up this series with its simple and direct title: 'The Theology of Pope Francis'.

They can be read independently of one another, obviously; they have been written by individual authors independently of each other. Nevertheless, the hope is that a reading of the entire series would not only be a valuable aid for grasping the theology upon which Francis' teaching is based, in the various theological fields of knowledge, but also an introduction to the key points of his thinking and teaching overall.

The intention, then, is not one of 'apologetics', and even less so is it to add further voices to the many already speaking about the Pope. The aim is to try to see, and to help others to see, what theological thinking Francis bases himself on and expresses, in such a fresh way in his teaching.

Among the many discoveries the reader could make in reading these volumes, would certainly be that of observing how so much of the beneficial freshness of the Council's teaching flows into Francis' magisterium. This is true both of the theological preparation he has had, and of what has followed from it. Given that it is perhaps still too soon for all this wealth to become common patrimony, peacefully and fully received by everyone, it should be no surprise that the Pope's teaching is sometimes not immediately understood by everyone.

By the same token, a point of no return has been reached in Francis' teaching, one that recent theology and the Council have both taught: that doctrine cannot be something extraneous to so-called pastoral theology and ministry. The truth that the Church is called to watch over is the truth of Christ's gospel, which needs to be communicated to the women and men of every time and place. This is why the task of the ecclesial magisterium must also be one of favouring this communication of the gospel. Hence, theology can never be reduced to a dry, desk-bound exercise, disconnected from the life of the people of God and its mission. This mission is that the women and men of every age encounter the perennial and inexhaustible freshness of Jesus' gospel.

Over these years there have been those who have heard some of Francis' own critical statements regarding theology or theologians, and have concluded that he holds it and them in low esteem. Perhaps a more detailed study of the Pope's teaching, such as offered by this series, could also be helpful for showing that, while we always need to be critical of a theology that loses its vital connection to the living faith of the Church, it is also essential to have a theology which takes up the task of thinking critically about this very faith, and doing so with 'creative fidelity', so that it may continue to be proclaimed.

Francis' teaching is certainly not lacking in a theology of this kind; and a theology of the kind is certainly one much desired by a magisterium such as his, which so wants God's mercy to continue to touch the minds and hearts of the women and men of our time.

Editor-in-chief
ROBERTO REPOLE

CONTENTS

Abbreviations 4

Preface to the Series 5

Introduction 13

Chapter 1

IGNATIUS OF LOYOLA AND THE 'MORE' OF THE GOSPEL IN A POPE WHOM WE CALL FRANCIS 15

1. *The gospel 'sine glossa'* 15
2. *"Nuestro modo de proceder"* 18
3. *"Contemplatives in action"* 21
4. *Discernment in the Spirit* 26
5. *Poverty as 'forma Ecclesia' and 'forma missionis'* 30

Chapter 2

CREATIVE FIDELITY: THEOLOGICAL TRADITION, VATICAN II, REINTERPRETING THE GOSPEL FOR TODAY 35

1. *In the spirit of Thomas Aquinas* 35
2. *Augustine and the primacy of grace and charity* 37
3. *Basil the Great and the Holy Spirit: architect of harmony* 42
4. *The perennial pillars of St Thomas' theology* .. 44

5. *St Bonaventure and the 'vestiges' of the Trinity* 48

6. *Precursors of renewal and Romano Guardini* 50

7. *Vatican II and Paul VI* 57

8. *The road taken by the Church and theology in Latin America and Argentina, and the Aparecida Document* 62

Chapter 3

Speaking of God today as he speaks through the gospel of Jesus 69

1. *Reform thinking* 69

2. *The encounter with Jesus Christ as principle and measure* 71

3. *At the heart of the kerygma with a new language* 75

4. *Flesh and mystery* 80

5. *Time as kairos and process* 83

6. *Harmonizing differences* 85

Chapter 4

Joyfully following the gospel to 'bring new relationships' into the world 87

1. *With the Easter Christ at the heart of the world* 87

2. *Mediating the 'new creation'* 89

3. *Flesh is God's way* 90

4. *Hearts opened wide*.. 93
5. *The sense of mystery*...................................... 96
6. *Having the same mind as Jesus and acting as Jesus would* 99

Chapter 5

FOUR WORDS TO REFORM THE CHURCH 103

1. *The Church, a people at the service of the coming of the Kingdom of God* 103
2. *'The medicine of mercy'* 107
3. *Synodality: what God expects of his Church* 112
4. *'A poor Church for the poor'* 115
5. *The prophecy of the 'culture of encounter'* 117

INTRODUCTION

Discovering the sources of Pope Francis' thinking has a fascination all of its own, because it is not about indulging in a detached and dry study. Rather is it a matter of immersing oneself in a life in which a tender and strong love for Christ, the Church, everyone and each individually, beginning with the poor and the disregarded, is on the lookout for how God is with his people, then highlights it, follows it and helps others to follow it.

It might seem anything but an easy undertaking at first sight, but in doing so one feels that one has encountered the Lord who is alive in the heart of a man whom his grace has called to be the Bishop of Rome and hence Pastor of the universal Church. Here we find the light of the gospel reflected in myriad ways through the experience and understanding of the faith across the centuries as it has matured in those who knew and followed Jesus, but also in those who have awaited him and longed for him and have in some way shared something of his message and life, even without knowing they were doing so.

Pope Francis' theology is an ecclesial but also existential theology, one which is spiritual and kerygmatic, mystical and social. It is an original and very personal synthesis that is very appealing and cogent, as shown by the joy and effectiveness it radiates.

Hence the method I have spontaneously followed in writing these pages: beginning with Ignatius of Loyola and Francis of Assisi, keen interpreters of Jesus' gospel in the Church's mission (Chapter 1), then moving on to the theological tradition illustrated by witnesses whom I have noticed are Pope Francis' preferred choice (Chapter 2), finally spending time with some of the more important theological directions – regarding God, the human being, the Church – we find in his magisterium (Chapters 3 to 5).

Chapter 1
IGNATIUS OF LOYOLA
AND THE 'MORE' OF THE GOSPEL
IN A POPE WHOM WE CALL FRANCIS

1. *The gospel* 'sine glossa'

We are struck by a statement in *Evangelii Gaudium* (*EG*) which seems to be just a throwaway line, but instead – if we meditate and accept what it really wants to say – shows that it carries quite some heft, including for someone who is exercising the ministry of the successor of Peter.

Pope Francis speaks of evangelization with the Spirit and invites us to look at Jesus so we can conform to his style in how we relate to others in the light of the Father, whether these others are companions on the journey in faith or in the human community, regardless of any labels or unseemly boundaries. He has this to say:

> This is not an idea of the Pope, or one pastoral option among others; they are injunctions contained in the word of God which are so clear, direct and convincing that they need no interpretations which might diminish their power to challenge us. Let us live them *sine glossa*, without commentaries. By so doing we will know the missionary joy of sharing life with God's faithful people as we strive to light a fire in the heart of the world (*EG* 271).

I would say that this is the real Pope Francis: his program and pastoral style certainly, but also the beating heart of his experience and understanding of the faith. Experience and understanding. Yes: when we listen to his teaching and are in harmony with Pope Francis's guidance, what does not leave us unaffected is that it is a penetrating experience of faith from which emerges a clear understanding of how the event which is Jesus Christ becomes history in the human story through the Church's ministry.

It is in the gospel, then, that we need to look, as it is the original and ongoing source of the peculiar style which informs Pope Francis' ministry. The gospel, obviously, as received from the Church's hands, faithfully guarded, interpreted and creatively embodied across the centuries by the Church's living tradition. The gospel, just like that, accepted, lived, proclaimed in its freshness and relevance, as it comes to us through the Church's mediation – 'holy Mother Church as hierarchy' as Francis likes to call it, following St Ignatius of Loyola.[1]

In this access to the gospel in today's Church and world, what strikes us is the fact that Jorge Mario Bergoglio is the first Jesuit Pope in history. A spiritual son of Saint Ignatius, then, called to exercise the ministry of unity, guidance and confirmation in the faith which we know to be so important for the Society of Jesus. This is no simple detail if we want

---

1   Cf. W Kasper, *Il Vangelo: origine, fondamento e fonte della gioia*, in *Papa Francesco. La rivoluzione della tenerezza e dell'amore*, Queriniana, Brescia 2015, pp. 37-47. (The work exists in English as *The Revolution of Tenderness and Love. Theological and Pastoral Perspectives*, Paulist Press; Translation edition, March 6, 2015).

to be in tune with the wavelength which inspires Pope Francis' interpretation and manner of carrying out the Petrine ministry. Because – as well illustrated by Vatican II's Constitution on Divine Revelation, *Dei Verbum* (*DV*) – understanding and putting the gospel into practice *proficit*, goes ahead and grows:

> in the Church with the help of the Holy Spirit. (5) For there is a growth in the understanding of the realities and the words which have been handed down. This happens through the contemplation and study made by believers, who treasure these things in their hearts (see Luke, 2:19, 51) through a penetrating understanding of the spiritual realities which they experience, and through the preaching of those who have received through Episcopal succession the sure gift of truth. For as the centuries succeed one another, the Church constantly moves forward toward the fullness of divine truth until the words of God reach their complete fulfilment in her (cf. no. 8).

Seen this way, one can appreciate how much the charism of St Ignatius – undoubtedly one of the *praeclara charismata* (extraordinary gifts) of which the Vatican Constitution on the Church, *Lumen Gentium* (*LG*), speaks (cf. no. 12) when pointing to the sources of experience and spiritual understanding of the faith for the People of God referred to in *DV* – offers Pope Francis as a pertinent and privileged way of accessing the beating heart of the gospel. This charism has been unremitting in its action through history, and is more than ever effective today. Is not the Society of Jesus called the '*via ad Illum*' in Julius 1II's Formula?[2]

2. "*Nuestro modo de proceder*"

Without doubt there is a virtuous circle that is established, spontaneously but with great fruitfulness, in the experience and understanding of the faith that animates Pope Francis' ministry. And, to put it in gospel terms, it is such that what he suggests to the Church by listening to the Spirit is based on the rock of the Word of God (cf. Mt 7:24), listened to and accepted for what it is: 'not as a human word but as what it really is, God's word' (1 Thess 2:13), as keen and effective as a double-edged sword, piercing until it divides body and soul (cf. Heb 4:12). The virtuous circle runs between acknowledgement of the Word of God in Scripture and its resonance today, here, for us, through the power of the Holy Spirit.

On the one hand it is from the Word – made flesh and lifted up on the cross in Christ Jesus – that the Holy Spirit who gives life is released once and for all, without measure and always afresh; but on the other hand it is only thanks to the gift of the Holy Spirit that the Word is remembered, understood in all its richness, and penetrates so we can grasp its marrow and communicate its beauty and truth (cf. Jn 14:26; 15:27; 16:8; 16:12-15).

This is the virtuous circle within which flows the rhythm of Christian life and the Church's mission, such that the

---

2   *Form. Inst. Jul. III*, no. 1.

Word of God which took flesh in Mary's womb through the work of the Holy Spirit may continue to take flesh by virtue of the same Holy Spirit in the story of humanity, until Christ truly becomes 'all in all' (cf. Col 3:11; 1 Cor 15:28). Christian truth, which is life for the world, has consolidated over the years, developed over time, been more thoroughly explored with age as indicated by the treatise of St Vincent of Lérins in his *Commonitorium*, which Pope Francis often refers to.[3]

St Ignatius of Loyola, through the impulse of the Spirit, traced out a luminous and robust path along this journey for the Church's mission in the unprecedented and challenging time of modernity. History does not happen with 'ifs' and 'buts'; and yet we cannot fail to consider, with a hint of dismay, what would have happened to the Catholic Church if the work of the Society of Jesus had not unfolded within it, given the demanding shift which was the era of modernity which only now in our time seems to be opening up to a new era.

At all levels: from mission to formation of the clergy, from academic culture to the arts, from scientific research to social action. What St Ignatius spelt out in such detail, starting with a rigorous and ongoing effort to listen to the will of God, is a 'way of proceeding'[4]: a way of ecclesial conformation to Christ's mission which Christ passed on to his Church in obedience to the Father for the salvation of the world.

---

3 *Commonitorium primum*, 23: PL 50,668.
4 "This Institute or way of proceeding, as Father Ignatius calls it ...": NADAL *3a Predica di Alcalà* (3rd Sermon at Alacalà 1561) in *Comm. De Inst* 304.

Is not the question of method at a philosophical (Descartes) and scientific (Galileo) level the *quaestio princeps* of modernity? And is it not above all with regard to the anthropological shift toward the subject (person), from the crucial standpoint of the meaning and destiny of freedom, that the decisive demands of truth and good, of individual dignity and where history is heading, come into play?

'Nuestro modo de proceder'. This is the 'method' that Jorge Mario Bergoglio chose and made his own from the moment he followed his inner urge to enter the Society of Jesus. This method – without exclusivity, it is obvious, and always in the context of the grand and well-developed tradition of the Church – has given him a valuable key for accessing the gospel in the demanding interpretation of life as a sharing in and expression of the mission of Christ's Church. I believe we need to go back to this method to fully understand and evaluate the style of his ministry as Bishop of Rome, what underpins it and the gift it represents for the Church.[5]

A method, mind you, because its content and objective are the same as always: witnessing to and igniting the 'fire of the Gospel' at the heart of today's world. He is convinced that a new stage has opened in the history of the Church's evangelization (cf. *EG* 17). And this spiritual outlook has the support of the magisterium of the Second Vatican Council and recent popes and is further corroborated by the journey

---

5   Cf. the lucid essay by A SPADARO, *La riforma della Chiesa secondo Francesco. Le radici ignaziane*, in *La Civiltà Cattolica*, no. 3968 (24 October 2105), pp. 114-131.

taken by the people of God in various parts of the world over recent decades.

3. "Contemplatives in action"

So, is the charism of Ignatius of Loyola a decisive source for the spiritual experience, thinking and ministry of Pope Bergoglio? And for that matter, 'which' Ignatius? Has not the history of the Society of Jesus known very many and sometimes discordant interpretations of its founder's charism?

An important factor comes into play here, beyond the strong personal sensitivity of the man and the Christian that is Jorge Mario Bergoglio, regarding the Ignatian experience and what it offers in terms of a blunt and costly evangelical approach. It is this: Vatican II, proposing an overall re-evaluation of the Church's mission by going back to its source and permanent norm in Jesus Christ, invited Religious Orders and Congregations to return to their original inspiration in order to undertake a creative and courageous updating for today's circumstances.[6] Only this way, effectively, could the virtuous circle between the Word and the Spirit which we spoke of earlier, get moving again, with a view to deciphering the 'signs of the times' in a relevant way and fully introducing the leaven of the gospel into the 'stuff' of human history. After all, the Council benefited more than a little from the contributions of great Jesuit theologians such as Henri de Lubac and Karl Rahner.

6   Cf. Decree *Perfectae Caritatis* on the renewal of religious life, no. 2.

As we know, this was also a bumpy road, including for the Society of Jesus. Jorge Mario Bergoglio, in many ways is a child and witness of this new season in the Church's life which prompted the Society of Jesus to re-read the grace of its origins in order to throw light on its mission today. Of course, it was Fr Pedro Arruppe, Superior General of the Jesuits from 1965 to 1983 who was the grand architect setting this imposing work in motion. And although it has already produced substantial results, one can presume that it has greater and more beautiful ones in reserve still for the future. Indeed, one thinks spontaneously of ecclesial experiences like the one illustrated by Cardinal Carlo Maria Martini's ministry in Milan, or illustrated today by Pope Francis' ministry. They represent the real proof of the goodness and foresight of perspectives and directions coming from the Council.

So, the Ignatius who offers Jorge Mario Bergoglio his 'way of proceeding' in the experience and understanding of Christ, is the one who was rediscovered, so to speak, in the clear and robust mystical system which animates not only the *Spiritual Exercises* (*SE*) but – As Fr Arrupe writes – also and inseparably, 'the process of converting the original intuitions of the Cardoner and La Storta into institutional principles – which are nothing but the *Constitutions*.'[7] The

---

7   P ARRUPE s.j., *L'ispirazione trinitaria del carisma ignaziano*, no. 53 (8 February 1980), cf. H Alphonso, *Il rinnovamento appropriato. Del carisma dei jesuiti-ignaziano quale vissuto e proposto dal Padre Arrupe*, Apostolato della Preghiera, Rome 2009. This document is also in English, cf., *Studies in the Spirituality of Jesuits*, 33/3 May 2001.

Rahner brothers had already moved in this direction: Hugo, in a series of conferences on the *SE* and the *Constitutions*, Karl in his recall to the mystical source of the Ignatian vision.[8]

On different occasions,[9] Pope Francis has explicitly recalled individuals who have inspired him for their interpretation of the Ignatian charism, men who saw it as a wellspring for their lives and grasped its essential mystical dimension. In the first place Peter Faber, Ignatius' first companion, whom Francis canonized on 17 December 2013, emphasizing his 'true and deep desire "to be expanded in God": he was completely centred in God, and because of this he could go, in a spirit of obedience, often on foot, throughout Europe and with charm dialogue with everyone and proclaim the Gospel.'[10] So it is very significant that Pope Francis refers to other illustrious exponents of the mystical interpretation of the Ignatian charism, such as Louis Lallement and Jean-Joseph Surin in the 17th century, then more recently, Gaston Ferrard and Michel de Certeau in the 20th century.

---

8 Cf. H Rahner, *Ignatius von Loyola und das geschichtliche Werden seiner Frömmigkeit*, Styria Verlag, Graz-Salzburg-Wien 1947; K Rahner, *Discorso di sant'Ignazio ad un gesuita odierno*, in *Scienza e fede cristiana*, (Nuovi Saggi IX), It. trans, Paoline, Rome 1984, pp. 522-574.

9 Cf. for example A Spadaro, *Interview with Pope Francis* http://w2.vatican.va/content/francesco/en/speeches/2013/september/documents/papa-francesco_20130921_intervista-spadaro.html

10 Pope Francis, *Homily on the liturgical memorial of the Most Holy Name of Jesus*, Church of the Gesù, Rome, 3 January 2014.

In the end, it is a question of grasping the actual evangelizing value of the 'way of proceeding' drawn up by St Ignatius, which can be summed up in the formula he himself gave us: *contemplatives in action*, which pointed to the program and commitment of focusing on God, immersing oneself in God, adhering in faith to Jesus Christ, listening to the Holy Spirit daily, being filled with his light and strength while working *ad maiorum Dei gloriam* in human history. It is about seeing and summing up everything freely in Christ so that He, Christ, may ultimately hand over to the Father everything the Father has created and redeemed, now that it has been transfigured.

Contemplatives in action. This Ignatian formula, on closer inspection, seems to lead to a fulfilment of an intent that has always been the energy behind the Church's mission and history, but is at the same time unprecedented and anticipated. Contemplation of God in Christ is the *incipit* and the *cantus firmus* of Christian experience, as stated by the prologue to the Fourth Gospel: 'and we have seen [*contemplated*] his glory, the glory as of a father's only son, full of grace and truth' (Jn 1:14). But *this* contemplation, precisely inasmuch as it introduces us, through the Word incarnate, to the depths of God (cf. 1 Cor 2:10-16), has us share in the Father's gaze of love through his Word on the world. And this involves the disciple, by faith, in his own mission: 'As the Father has sent me, so I send you ... Receive the Holy Spirit' (Jn 20:21-22).

Contemplation of God in Christ, then, does not lead to obscurity, fogginess, but passes through it, through the night of the Crucifixion, reaching the unfading light of the thrice holy God to then communicate it, incarnate it in the days and works of men and women. At the heart of the Medieval period – which was the dawning of modernity, prepared for by the extraordinary work of inculturation of the faith set in motion by the Fathers of the Church – was this great intuition of Saints Francis and Dominic, each in his own way: *contemplata aliis tradere*, passing on the more intense and tasty fruits of contemplating God for everyone, at the heart of the 'city of man'. For St Francis it was a case of conforming himself to the crucified Christ even to the extent of receiving the stigmata in his own body, Christ's passion whose wounds continue to be seen in the flesh of humankind today.

This was the 'way of proceeding' which Ignatius made his own. As the Archbishop of Buenos Aires, Jorge Mario Bergoglio wrote that:

> like Saint Teresa, [he] understands that the only secure access to the divinity is the most holy humanity of our Lord. And, speaking of the passion, we need to delve into this humanity, this man Jesus who is God but who suffers as a man in his own body, his own psyche. This is no folktale but a real story, the only tangible way along which we must all travel in order to contemplate the Father who reveals himself through the Son. We will contemplate the passion in the flesh of Jesus, in our flesh. There is no other way if we want to really profess that

Jesus is alive, risen in his own flesh, with wounds open and the transcendence of the Father's face.[11]

4. Discernment in the Spirit

Not only does the formula *contemplatives in action* trace the circular existential (and theological) route between union with God and service of humankind, indissolubly linked in Christ who is both divine and human; it also identifies and proposes the method which acts as the hinge between the two, constantly ferrying understanding and decision from one to the other: discernment in the Spirit. This is the key term which embraces both the core of the Ignatian charism and the theological and pastoral style of Pope Francis.

This is not a technique we are talking about but a way – in experience and understanding of the faith – of sharing in Christ's mission in the Church. There is nothing private and individualistic in the demanding art of discernment as St Ignatius portrays it, even though – and it is obvious, from the perspective of anthropology enlightened by Jesus Christ

---

11 JM BERGOGLIO (Pope Francis), *Aprite la mente al vostro cuore*, Rizzoli, Milan 2013, p. 235 (English Edition, *Open Mind, Faithful Heart. Reflections on Following Jesus*, The Crossroad Publishing Company, Reprint Edition September 15, 2015). With regard to St Teresa of Avila, St John of the Cross, St Teresa of the Child Jesus – the three Carmelite Doctors of the Church – we need to remember that a reference text for the spirituality and theology of Pope Francis is, of course, the extraordinary book by P. MARIE-EUGÉNE DE L'ENFANT JÉSUS, *Je veux voir Dieu* (published in two volumes then later as one, in 1949 and 1951, whose author Pope Francis beatified in 2016).

– discernment appeals to and involves the core and destiny of the individual like nothing else does. But it is carried out in Christ, with the Church, for humankind. The point is to discover one's mission in the mission of Christ within the Church and at the service of humankind. Then, step by step, event after event, to discover in each circumstance – by listening to the Spirit – the decision which has to be taken and the path to concretely follow. Discernment is a work which is very personal but at the same time, communal and ecclesial. Did not St Ignatius encourage us to *sentire cum Ecclesia*?

This is not just an added, external feature but part of the very nature of discernment, insofar as it is the 'way of proceeding' through which, through the mission of the Spirit, the disciple of Christ is clear about the direction taken in discipleship in the context of the mission of the Church in the here and now of humanity's history. The soul which is forged in the crucible of discernment becomes in truth – to put it as the Fathers of the Church did – 'an ecclesial soul'. So much so that the adjective 'communal' (or 'communitarian') which today seems to be much closer to the noun 'discernment', could even seem redundant.

In fact, discernment of its nature implies the ecclesial community. If there is one good reason for making this essential dimension explicit today, it goes back to the need to learn how to follow the paths for putting into practice the ecclesiology drawn up by Vatican II, the ecclesiology of the people of God and communion for mission. It must be clear that to avoid this ecclesiology just remaining an intention on paper, there is a need for times and places and especially for learning a method all of which allow us to work as a community, involve everyone and everyone's gifts and ministries working in harmony, and manage the Church's mission at the various levels at which it is expressed – local, regional, universal.

Basically, when Pope Francis says with foresight and decision that 'what the Lord is asking of us is already in some sense present in the very word "synod"'[12] he is not only committing the Church to a courageous step forward in carrying out the mission indicated by Vatican II, but is carrying out God's plan for the Church of Christ as we find in the pages of the New Testament and as gradually outlined by the *Traditio vivens* of the Church. He does so by capitalizing on the great gift that the Ignatian charism has given focus to in the patrimony of the Christian faith.

This too is a theological and ecclesiological gain resulting from Vatican II. As remarked in the recent document from the Congregation for the Doctrine of the Faith, *Iuvenescit Ecclesia*, while there is no doubt that from the beginning of its history the Church has experienced the active and fertile presence, in its midst and in its mission, of even extraordinary charisms of the Holy Spirit which have helped integrate and corroborate the irreplaceable role and activity of the ordained minister, it is only on the basis of the teaching of Vatican II that we have come to recognize that 'hierarchical

---

12 Cf POPE FRANCIS, *Address commemorating the 50th anniversary of the institution of the Synod of Bishops*, Paul VI Hall, 17 October 2015.

and charismatic gifts' are 'co-essential' in the life and journey of the Church.[13]

As an example, and it is not simply one example among many but carries particular and perhaps even decisive weight, the interpretation of the 'signs of the times' entrusted to the whole People of God by Vatican II, in the language employed by the Pastoral Constitution of the Church in today's world, *Gaudium et Spes* (*GS*, nos 11 and 44), asks precisely for the exercise of *community discernment* which, on the one hand, is illuminated by the Word of God and, on the other, and thanks to it, allows us to distinguish the true signs of the Spirit of God in the occasions, problems, challenges, conquests and even the abuses of our time: the Spirit of God who renews the face of the earth (cf. no. 26).

So there is a need – as Pope Francis write in *EG* – to become contemplatives of the Word and the people (cf. no. 154), which means having the eyes of the soul wide open toward the horizons of infinity disclosed by the Spirit, and at the same time being committed with all our being to managing everyday reality. *Non coerceri a maximo, contineri tamen a minimo, divinum est:* not to be confined by the greatest but to be contained within the smallest, this is divine – written by an anonymous Jesuit in honour of St Ignatius. It seems to capture the spirit and style of Pope Francis.

---

13 Cf. CONGREGATION FOR THE DOCTRINE OF THE FAITH, Letter on the relationship between hierarchical and charismatic gifts for the life and mission of the Church *Iuvescit Ecclesia*, 15 May 2016.

5. *Poverty as* 'forma Ecclesia' *and* 'forma missionis'

But it is not only the charism of Ignatius of Loyola which inspires, and I would add, stimulates his ministry. There is the entire great spiritual tradition of the Church which flows into the teaching of Ignatius and comes from it in turn, re-proposed and updated with its own peculiar perspective. After all, this is how it always happens in the Church: every great charism is not a lonely monad standing apart but fits directly and indirectly into the concert which is the ecclesial symphony. All the charisms share the same source which is the Holy Spirit.

Of course there is another extraordinary charism which, in its own way, gives life to the experience and understanding of faith as expressed in the ministry of Pope Bergoglio: the charism of Saint Francis of Assisi. The very fact that he, the first Jesuit Pope in history, felt urged to choose this name among all others at the moment of his election to the Chair of Peter, says a lot about his way of living and understanding the *sequela Christi* and exercising the ministry which God's grace has called him to. This symptomatic choice has more to it than just the dream of 'a poor Church for the poor' as we find in *EG* (no. 198), nor is it just the willingness to bring a commitment to the fore to something that just cannot be put off any longer – care for our common home, as illustrated by *Laudato Si'* (*LS*). In my opinion, in the light of the charism of St Francis, and on a par with what he has taken from St Ignatius, he goes to the heart of the experience and understanding of the gospel.

The poor Christ, who empties himself of everything, even his equality in divinity with the Father (cf. Phil 2:7), to enrich us through his poverty (cf. 1 Cor 8:9), is God's way to us and our way to God, and our way to others. This is the 'new and living' way (Heb 10:19-20) that Francis of Assisi received as a gift from the Spirit and offered the Church: '*Nemo intrat recte in Deum nisi per Crucifixum*', as we find in St Bonaventure's *Itinerarium*, pointing out the *Poverello* to everyone as an *exemplum verae contemplationis*.[14] It is a contemplation rooted in sharing in Christ's poverty and is the source of universal fellowship with men and women, animals, plants and all inanimate things, as St Francis sings in his *Canticle of Brother Sun*.

St Ignatius himself, when he was caught up in the important work of writing the Constitutions (important because they would give the final shape to the Society of Jesus, according to divine inspiration) confirms the will to follow Christ in his absolute poverty without renouncing the 'offering of greater importance.'[15] 'Imitating him in putting up with every kind of poverty, real and spiritual.' As Fr Arrupe has shown, beginning from Ignatius' *Diary* (February 1544 – February 1545), this is why he immersed himself in contemplation of the most dizzying mystery of God which faith in Christ introduces us to, that of the Blessed Trinity, finally finding there the confirmation he

---

14 BONAVENTURE FROM BAGNOREGIO, *Itinerarium mentis in Deum*, Prologus, 3: 'In truth, no one enters into God unless through the Crucifix.'

15 *SE*, no. 98.

yearned for with all his being: 'The Son first of all sent the apostles to preach in poverty, then the Holy Spirit confirmed them by giving them his own strength in tongues of fire; thus, from the moment that the Father and the Son sent the Holy Spirit, all three divine Persons approved that manner of sending.'[16]

Poverty, then, received by Christ, as Dante Alighieri would say, as 'his dearest Lady'[17] was accepted and chosen as such by St Francis and St Ignatius in the name of the Church as *forma missionis*, the main and essential form of the Church's mission following in the footsteps of the poor and crucified Christ. This is a perspective that *LG*, in no. 8, makes its own with a broad and well-developed description I am including here in its entirety, because it is crucial for interpreting the inspiration which gives life to Pope Francis' ministry:

> Just as Christ carried out the work of redemption in poverty and persecution, so the Church is called to follow the same route that it might communicate the fruits of salvation to men. Christ Jesus, "though He was by nature God . . . emptied Himself, taking the nature of a slave" (Phil 2:6-7), and "being rich, became poor" (2 Cor 8:9) for our sakes. Thus, the Church, although it needs human resources to carry out its mission, is not set up to seek earthly glory, but to proclaim, even by its own example, humility

16 *Diary*, 11 February 1544
17 Cf. *Divine Comedy, Paradise*, Canto XI.

and self-sacrifice. Christ was sent by the Father "to bring good news to the poor, to heal the contrite of heart" (Lk 4:18), "to seek and to save what was lost" (Lk 19:10). Similarly, the Church encompasses with love all who are afflicted with human suffering and in the poor and afflicted sees the image of its poor and suffering Founder. It does all it can to relieve their need and in them it strives to serve Christ … The Church, "like a stranger in a foreign land, presses forward amid the persecutions of the world and the consolations of God", announcing the cross and death of the Lord until He comes"(cf. 1 Cor 11:26) By the power of the risen Lord it is given strength that it might, in patience and in love, overcome its sorrows and its challenges, both within itself and from without, and that it might reveal to the world, faithfully though darkly, the mystery of its Lord until, in the end, it will be manifested in full light.

In these words – charismatically prepared and formulated – there is a leap in quality in the Church's awareness of itself and its mission. But only when this statement has begun to reawaken ecclesial awareness and become flesh and blood in the pastoral life of the Church – I am thinking in particular of the journey taken by the people of God in Latin America – will it begin to perceive and gauge its theological, ecclesial, social and cultural import.

Pope Francis' magisterium heads in this by now essential direction, and does so with clarity and vigour.

Chapter 2
CREATIVE FIDELITY:
THEOLOGICAL TRADITION, VATICAN II,
REINTERPRETING THE GOSPEL FOR TODAY

1. In the spirit of Thomas Aquinas

It is a fact that St Thomas Aquinas is the theologian who is far more present in *Amoris Laetitia* (*AL*) but also in *Evangelii Gaudium* (*EG*). With all due respect to those who appeal to a rigid and fossilized interpretation of the *Doctor communis*, it is difficult to grasp the spirit and the inspiration behind this other than by precise references to one or other passage.

Thomas is an extraordinarily alive and relevant theologian, and it is no coincidence that *Optatum Totius*, Vatican II's Decree on priestly formation, held him up as a sure guide for an ecclesially responsible and fruitful theological ministry. This may not be the case for all the contributions he has given or for all his claims (how could it be?) but it certainly is the case for his intention and the basic methodology that inspires his work.

It might seem obvious, though not always, to say that Thomas is not a dyed-in-the-wool Thomist! He is a flexible and open theologian (and philosopher) in whom fidelity to the *depositum fidei* and creativity in discerning the most suitable conceptual language are harmoniously combined.

And it cost him something to achieve this. He paid attention to the truth and the signs of the times in order to express the message of Revelation to the people of his day in an intelligible and appreciable way. To be aware of this it is sufficient to re-read studies by people like Marie-Dominique Chenu[1] or Jean-Pierre Torrell,[2] who have helped to reinstate the relevance of Aquinas and his contribution in its cultural context so as to savour its genuine inspiration.

It is no coincidence, then, that Thomas Aquinas is also a sure theological reference point for Pope Francis, and not only because the Society of Jesus has always engaged in continuous reinterpretation and updating of his teaching – in the very spirit of Thomas himself. Nor is it only because Thomas' theology was a keystone of formation in the theological studies imparted in Argentina before and after the Council. But, I say once more, it is his attitude of listening, in the freedom that comes from the Spirit, to the essential things Aquinas continues to teach us about doing theology.

And it is precisely because of this intelligent and open fidelity to the theology of Thomas Aquinas that the theology which nurtures and guides the ministry of Pope Francis exhibits two specific characteristics which stand out if one looks at his sources: one is the very many references, hence not just the monotony of one author and a single school, but

---

[1] MD Chenu, *St. Thomas d'Aquin et la théologie*, Editions du Seuil, Paris 1959.

[2] J-P Torrell, *Imitation à Saint Thomas d'Aquin. Sa personne et son œuvre*, Editions Universitaires, Fribourg Suisse 1993.

a broad symphony of voices from the Church's experience, a whole spectrum of references and interests ranging from the Fathers of the Church, through the Medieval period and on to modernity, right up to our own times, without limiting himself to professional theologians but including 'secular styles' as von Balthasar puts it. These latter deal with the truths of the gospel in the language of literature, the arts, sciences. The other is his adoption of the magisterium of the Second Vatican Council as a key to interpretation of the patrimony which has been conserved and transmitted by tradition, and of the faith as it is presently experienced. This key to interpretation is not a final point of arrival but a promising launching pad.

2. *Augustine and the primacy of grace and charity*

Of the Fathers of the Church, the one dearest to Pope Francis is St Augustine of Hippo, and not just from a literary point of view: in the sense that the perennial modernity of his human and spiritual style could only but appeal to the cultivated artistic temperament of the young Jorge Mario Bergoglio. It is enough to think of the inimitable music of the spirit which echoes through the *Confessions*. And yet there is something else: Augustine's journey, which is a parable of the existential seeking done by human beings of any age and place, driven patiently and wisely by God himself who makes himself present, attracts, forgives, welcomes, seeks out, sends us to others. If there is one word that sums up Augustine's journey and which returns in the definition of the theology which takes its inspiration from him – a word dear to Pope Francis and which expresses how he feels about the breath of Christian life – it is the verb *quaerere*, to seek, look for.

It is a true and real seeking, thus a poignant and unsettling one as it explores the mystery of existence and the horizon this existence stands out from, but at the same time it is a seeking that sets out and keeps going because it has always perceived somehow that the goal it seeks, the arrival point it is aiming at, the quiet it yearns for, are no chimera or illusion but a reality, 'the' reality. '*Chaque soif a son eau.*' Every thirst has its water.

It is true on the one hand – as Augustine writes – that '*inquietum est cor nostrum donec requiescat in te,*' our hearts are restless until they rest in you, but it is just as true that the *quies* which the *quaerere* achieves, animated by the infinite *desiderium* within the human being, is far different from tranquil possession gained once and for all and which exempts one from continuing the search.

Hence the other wonderful formula in which Augustine sums up the energy of existence seen in terms of faith: '*Quaeramus inveniendum, quaeramus inventum. Ut inveniendus quaeratur occultus est; ut inventus quaeratur, immensus est,*' which can be translated as follows: we must seek it out to find it, and we must continue to seek it out even when we have found it. So let us seek to find it because it is hidden; let us seek it out even when we have found it because it is immense.[3] If *fides* is the response of grace to the

3   *In Johannis Evangelium*, LXIII, 1.

quaerere of infinite human desire, in and of itself it gives rise to a further *quaerere* that is one with the existence of faith which, if it has an intellectual dimension, runs through all the other dimensions of human experience. Thus we have the true meaning of theology: not possessing the truth but being possessed by the Truth which gives itself and which, in the Holy Spirit, invites and guides us to journey toward its fullness. *Fides quaerens intellectum, fides* that is *desiderium videndi quod credidi.*[4]

The lesson from Augustine who is – and let us not forget this – both theologian and pastor, a pastor with the smell of the sheep, as evidenced even from reading the homilies written down by the faithful who were listening to him, is a lesson which accompanies the spiritual, pastoral and theological journey of Jorge Mario Bergoglio. It is a lesson in which, perhaps, the two pearls of evangelical wisdom which the great Bishop and Doctor of Hippo gifts us with shine out: grace and charity.

Grace first of all. It seems to me that his perception of the mystery of grace is decisive for Augustine's existential and pastoral performance on the one hand, but also for Pope Francis' performance on the other, and shapes his *Weltanschauung* from head to toe, meaning his outlook and access to the ultimate meaning of reality in Christ. As evidenced especially by the eighth Book of the *Confessions*, where Augustine tells the story of his conversion, Christ's grace breaks through suddenly (even if it is always expected)

---

4   Cf. Augustine, *De Trinitate*, XV, 28.51.

in the wounded and turbulent events of our life and makes it possible for us to make a free decision which life of itself could not produce, and which, once it is given as a gift, opens us up to the experience of a new and mysterious synergy which is alive and effective, between the movements that come from God and the discernment in life's journey that comes from the human heart.

These are pages that describe like few others the mystery, energy, the fruits of encounter with the grace of Christ which the apostle Paul speaks of in unforgettable words in the Letter to the Romans, and which Maurice Blondel refers to in his phenomenology of existence, *L'Action*. It is no coincidence that here is another author dear to Pope Francis.

From here, I think, from this fundamental experience and understanding of the event of grace for us, comes the recurring warning in his magisterium against the ongoing temptation of Pelagianism. It was Augustine in the first place, and in paradigmatic form, who firmly warned the Church against this.

To presume that I can do without the grace of Christ, even if this is not stated by way of principle, but appears to be the case from how I manage my life and the Church's mission, not only means that I do not recognize who I am and who God is in my personal and community existence, and not only means that I am unaware of the sin from which Christ redeems us, and that I am forgetting the gratitude expressed in faith for this unpayable debt, but it also means going astray where the decisive criterion of evangelization is concerned: the content and form in which the joyful proclamation of the gospel must be communicated and passed on – with mercy and tenderness. 'You received without payment; give without payment' (Mt 10:8).

Hence the other pearl which shines out in Augustine's lesson, and that draws directly on the teaching of the New Testament, especially in the First Letter of John: charity. Charity – *agápe*, in the New Testament lexicon – not as one attribute among many of God's that has been revealed to us and passed on eschatologically in Christ, but as the very essence of his mystery. As a consequence, charity as the quality which determines the new life of the disciple of Christ which, by definition, is *ho agapón*, one who loves: because one has first been loved by God, in Christ, and therefore by way of response, one is called to love one's brothers and sisters by taking the first step.

As he never tires of repeating through word and gesture, Pope Francis draws an *ontology of grace* from the Jesus event, an experience of new life completely characterized by the gift of God and expressed in a demanding and liberating *ethos of charity* that exhibits a combined personal and social dimension, a spiritual root, and is politically effective.

Augustine, Doctor of grace and charity, not surprisingly has given the Church two irreplaceable works: in the first, *De Trinitate*, he contemplates the unfathomable mystery of God who is Love and who inhabits both the *interiore homine* and *caritas ad invicem*; in the second, *De Civitatis Dei*, he reinterprets the history of humanity and its eschatological destiny in the light of the agapaic principle in the dialectic between *amor sui* and *amor Dei*.

The Church's social magisterium, basically, evolves this principle for practical situations. I am thinking, for example, of what *Gaudium et Spes* (*GS*) says in no. 24, where it proposes a daring similarity between the unity of love of the three divine persons and unity in truth and charity between the children of God, emphasizing that this shows that 'man, who is the only creature on earth which God willed for itself, cannot fully find himself except through a sincere gift of himself.' Pope Francis sums up the intuition of the social relevance of Christian faith by making his own a statement from the *Compendium of the Social Doctrine of the Church*: 'God, in Christ, redeems not only the individual person, but also the social relations existing between men' (*EG* 178).

3. Basil the Great and the Holy Spirit: architect of harmony

Augustine is not the only one of the Fathers of the Church who are an inspiration for Pope Francis' magisterium. Other than explicit references, we are talking about a style, an understanding and a way of proposing the central and crucial content of the Christian message in a language and with emphases that make it trenchant and worthy of appreciation today. Among the Fathers of the Church who set off Pope Francis' experience and understanding of the faith in a special way, it is enough to recall Basil the Great and his theology of the Holy Spirit.

If we examine Pope Bergoglio's major texts carefully and in detail, but also his more ordinary interventions in catechesis and liturgy, and if we set about interpreting the deeper meaning of his pastoral choices and gestures, it is not difficult to see the constant and crucial reference to the action of the Holy Spirit in the Church's mission. After all, it is precisely the article of faith concerning the Holy Spirit in the Nicene-Constantinopolitan Creed which introduces the article of faith on the Church and the eschatological destiny of creation.

If someone, rightly, has been able to complain about a certain lack of pneumatology in the dictates of Vatican II, then the pontifical magisterium which followed – I am thinking above all of *Dominum et Vivificantum* by John Paul II – sees this lack being gradually overcome, also undoubtedly due to the beneficial influence of the spirituality and theology of Eastern Christianity. Thus the hope expressed by Pope John – that the Council would be a 'new Pentecost' for the Church – is being apparently realized little by little in the history of its reception and its effects. Pope Francis' magisterium is undoubtedly a confirmation of this and a further powerful impulse in this direction.

Basil the Great, to whom Pope Francis refers to illustrate the style of God's action in his (Basil's) great book on the Holy Spirit, *Peri tou Agiou Pneumatos*, offered the Church a work of charismatic substance and lasting significance. Among other things, it clearly stood out at the Second Ecumenical Council, Constantinople I, in that it produced, on the basis of Basil's theology, the Symbol of Faith that all Christians together still profess today. It should be noted that Basil the Great wrote his work only a few years before Augustine began writing *De Trinitate*. Hence there is also a temporal link between these two works which would remain fundamental in the illustration of the doctrine of faith.

What Pope Francis draws from Basil's work is not so much or only the statement regarding equality in the divinity – in God's trinitarian being – of the Holy Spirit with the Father and the Son, a central tenet of Christian faith, but the dynamics of his activity in the mission of the Church and the history of humanity. In fact the Holy Spirit 'blows where he chooses' (cf. Jn 3:8), disseminating the diversity of his gifts to enrich peoples, cultures, local Churches with every truth, goodness and beauty in order to lead them, through mutual recognition and the mutual exchange of gifts, to the unity of the one Body of Christ which Augustine would say is the *Christus totus*, Christ who is 'all in all things'. Thus, the Spirit is, at the same time the principle of multiplicity and the principle of unity, the principle, that is, of unity that is not monolithic but is harmony: symphony and reconciliation of differences.

A central truth of faith such as the divinizing activity of the Spirit of the Father and the Son allows Francis to call on the lesson of St Basil in illuminating, discerning and guiding the Church's mission according to a logic which is fundamentally theological and even trinitarian. And this with all the relevant implications it has for imagining this new stage of evangelization, and with the spiritual and pastoral conversion it implies.

4. *The perennial pillars of St Thomas' theology*

But let us move on quickly to the Middle Ages and then immediately to modernity. There are really no gaps or ideological oppositions involved in the world which Pope

Francis displays when he interprets, receives and evaluates the great theological tradition of the Church.

The perennially valid teaching of St Thomas Aquinas is one example. Other than the clear difference of psychological sensitivity and cultural context that distinguishes Aquinas' teaching from St Augustine's, Francis takes up the great inspirational principles of his work, precisely in the sense in which Thomas goes further than Augustine on many fronts, Francis is, however, aware of preserving and taking further advantage of it and developing its valuable and irreplaceable contributions. This too is a good criterion for healthy, open and creative tradition. If we look, then, at the general – let's call them architectural – features of Pope Francis' pastoral approach and journey, some of the key teachings of the *Doctor communis* are easily recognizable: they are not taken up as static dogmas, but as dynamic inspirational principles in harmony with the philosophical reinterpretation of Thomism, for example, by Alberto Methol Ferré, one of the more fertile and original Latin American intellectuals of last century and very much appreciated by Jorge Mario Bergoglio. I am thinking principally of the correlation between the ontology of grace and the ethos of charity which is the backbone of Thomas' *intelligentia fidei*. St Thomas takes special care to articulate the relationship between *gratia* and *natura*, according to the well-known *gratia non tollit sed supponit et perficit naturam*,[5] thus stating a principle which is still essential today for ensuring that

---

5   *S. Th.* I, 1, 8 ad 2: "grace does not destroy nature but perfects it."

evangelization combines effectively and relevantly with human development, proclamation, or in other words so that the heart of the gospel message is properly assumed into the dynamics and forms of personal and communal human existence.

I am thinking, secondly, of the principle of *caritas forma omnium virtutum*,[6] which, at the level of the concrete process of moral action, persuasively translates the lofty principle, derived directly from New Testament teaching, according to which the Holy Spirit himself is '*lex Novi Testamenti*.'[7] If the specific hermeneutic of moral action in Christ that Thomas offers is not adequately taken into account, one cannot penetrate the authentic and perfectly traditional teaching proposed by Pope Francis, for example, in *AL*. Nor can one grasp the constructive importance, including at a social level, of a vision of charity which is at the same time an inextricably personal virtue and personal relationship, in

---

6 *S. Th.* I-II, 62, 4: "Sic enim caritas est mater omnium virtutum et radix, inquantum est omnium virtutum forma (For thus charity is the mother and root of every virtue inasmuch as it is the form of all the virtues)."

7 *S. Th.* I-II, 106, 1: "unaquaeque res illud videtur esse quod in ea est potissimum, ut philosophus dicit, in IX Ethic. Id autem quod est potissimum in lege novi testamenti, et in quo tota virtus eius consistit, est gratia spiritus sancti, quae datur per fidem Christi. Et ideo principaliter lex nova est ipsa gratia spiritus sancti, quae datur Christi fidelibus ('Each thing appears to be that which preponderates in it,' as the Philosopher states (*Ethic.* ix, 8). 'Now that which is preponderant in the law of the New Testament, and whereon all its efficacy is based, is the grace of the Holy Ghost, which is given through faith in Christ. Consequently the New Law is chiefly the grace itself of the Holy Ghost, which is given to those who believe in Christ')."

other words the principle for true 'social transformation' as *GS* puts it in no. 38.[8] Benedict XVI, both in *Deus Caritas Est* and *Caritas in Veritate*, developed this specific perspective in theologically persuasive terms.

And finally, what would appear to be the very heart of Thomas' theology is preserved and passed on in Pope Francis' experience and understanding of the faith: the centrality of the Eucharistic mystery. Adoration and celebration of the Eucharist, for St Thomas, are the point of departure and arrival of Christian life and the Church's mission. When he speaks of the need for theology to be done 'on our knees' to be a genuine *opus Dei* in the service of the Church for the world – and this also reminds us of a statement by Hans Urs von Balthasar – Pope Francis is of course thinking of a lifestyle and way of thinking which describes Thomas' theological teaching. As the hagiographic tradition reminds us, did he not spend time in prayer before the Blessed Sacrament to receive light and inspiration from on high for what he then had to explore and write about the truths of faith? And did he not, after celebrating the Eucharist at St Dominic the Great in Naples on 6 December 1273 in which he '*mira*

---

8 "For God's Word, through Whom all things were made, was Himself made flesh and dwelt on the earth of men.(10) Thus He entered the world's history as a perfect man, taking that history up into Himself and summarizing it.(11) He Himself revealed to us that 'God is love' (1 John 4:8) and at the same time taught us that the new command of love was the basic law of human perfection and hence of the worlds transformation. To those, therefore, who believe in divine love, He gives assurance that the way of love lies open to men and that the effort to establish a universal brotherhood is not a hopeless one" (*GS* 38).

mutatione commotus', cease to write and dictate (and he was in the finishing stretch of writing the *Summa Theologiae*!), replying to his good friend Reginald who asked him why: 'I cannot ... I cannot, because everything I have written seems like straw to me compared to what I have seen and what has been revealed to me.'?[9]

It is no simple humility that urges Thomas to make this gesture and say these words. Or better, it is the true humility which speaks to the reality of things: the overwhelming mystery of God and the human calling, and the calling of creation to share, through the Eucharist, in his divine life. The *Res* of the sacrament of the Eucharist, in fact, as Thomas explains, is union with God, unity of all of us, in Christ Jesus.[10]

5. St Bonaventure and the 'vestiges' of the Trinity

But in looking at the great theology of the Middle Ages, among the sources of Pope Francis' thinking we need to recall is also St Bonventure from Bagnoregio, the Seraphic Doctor. Not just because he is one of and perhaps the most outstanding – along with Blessed Duns Scotus – of the theological consequences of the charism of St Francis, but also because St Bonaventure represents a new stage in theology in the Church's history. In other respects, Thomas Aquinas, the Angelic Doctor, had also been a new stage.

9   *Processus*, no. 79, 376 ff.
10   Cf. *S. Th.* III, 73, 2: "Eucharistia est sacramentum ecclesiasticae unitatis (the Eucharist is the sacrament of ecclesial unity)"; III, 73, 3: "Res sacramenti est unitas corporis mystici (the effect of this sacrament is the unity of the mystical body)".

Joseph Ratzinger illustrated this very well in his study of *The Theology of Saint Bonaventure*[11] and insisted on it once he became Pope. As he explained, until Bonaventure, people had been led to believe that the essentials of doctrine and theology arising from the gospel already lay behind them in the Church's history, expressed through the Councils in the early centuries and in the theology of the Fathers of the Church. The appearance of the mendicant Orders during the Middle ages, however, dealt the cards afresh. Given the special momentum of the charism of St Francis, and without losing anything of the valuable *depositum* of the tradition, people began to look ahead to the dynamic tension between fidelity and creativity. Indeed, Francis' experience of the stigmata at La Verna was – in the eyes of those who followed him – not only an *exemplum verae contemplationis*, but also an evocative and eloquent 'theological icon'.

Thus St Bonaventure, looking at the Crucified Lord of and in Francis, opened the way to a theology that is both affective and cosmic. It is affective because it comes from *com*-passion with the flesh of Christ and its extension in the flesh of his brothers and sisters. It is cosmic because it is aimed at marking out and harmonizing, by listening to the Spirit, the traces of the One and Triune God in all of creation in the song of his wonder and beauty and in the cry of his wounds. Hence we see the first traces of that trinitarian 'cosmovision' that sees the creative and redemptive force of God, Trinity of love, not only reflected, but present and

---

11 J Ratzinger *The Theology of History in St Bonaventure*, Franciscan Press June 1, 1971.

active in the relationship that weaves a single design out of a rainbow of colours, the White light – *Claritas* – which radiates on the world from the heart of God.

This inspiration of the theology of the Trinity and Franciscan theology gives light and colour to Pope Francis' *Laudato Si' (LS)*. It opens up horizons which we perceive to be fascinating and in practice also decisive for the future of humanity.

6. *Precursors of renewal and Romano Guardini*

In truth, as persuasively demonstrated by Johannes Baptist Metz in his *Christliche Anthropozentrik*[12] and Ghislain Lafont in his *Histoire théologique de l'Eglise Catholique*,[13] while Thomas Aquinas was fully a man and theologian of the Middle Ages, he was already modern or, at the very least, decisively pre-modern. His interpretation of the Christian faith is certainly theocentric but in doing so it puts the consistency of created and temporal things and the dignity of the human being at the centre and makes the most of them. This is a great work of inculturation of the gospel message in conceptual categories that make it possible for him to express the humanizing value he pursues to the utmost.

This is why Thomas was not afraid of making a daring choice that would allow him to achieve significant results

---

12 JB METZ *Christliche Anthropozentric*. Über die *Denkform des Thomas von Aquin*, Kösel, Munich 1962.
13 G LAFONT, *Histoire théologique de l'Eglise Catholique*, Editions du Cerf, Paris 1994.

which the Catholic Church would benefit from for a long time from the heart of the Middle Ages to the present day, and which would also attract harsh criticism and persistent misunderstanding, especially at the beginning. He made the choice of Aristotle, whom he had learned about from the time he was attending Federico II's *Studium* in Naples, as the main exponent of the *recta ratio* that *fides* is called to take up, redeem and illustrate. It was a choice of epic proportions, even just considering that Platonic philosophy, in its many variations, had been absolutely pre-eminent for centuries in exercising the *intelligentia fidei*. And while Plato – as painted by Raphael in his famous painting of the School of Athens in the Vatican – turns his gaze upwards to the contemplation of Ideas and Goodness, Aristotle looks down instead, to nature and the city.

Thomas Aquinas' strategic choice establishes what is most typical in Christian faith: the alliance with right reason which is called to open up and, so to speak, be transubstantiated in the purifying and illuminating light of Revelation, and also discernment of the signs of the times and the process of inculturation. Christian faith is faith in the Logos, yes, but in the Logos that became flesh and lived among us (cf. Jn 1:14). Also this side of Thomas is a precious guide and example for Pope Francis, just as it was for Vatican II which, paradoxically at first sight, made a clear break with the rigidity and sterile repetition of some ossified expressions which Neo-scholasticism took literally from his thought in its commitment to be faithful to the spirit of St Thomas.

The rapid and sometimes feverish onset of Modernity pushed theology and Christian inspiration to a profound renewal of its language and how it presented its message, so it could continue and in some cases recover its relationship with cultural and social currents gradually taking up the reins in society's journey. The sciences were born, knowledge became autonomous, the technical world was affirmed, the 'new world' was discovered ... As already mentioned in the previous chapter, for this immense task the experience and understanding of the faith in the Catholic Church between the sixteenth and seventeenth centuries, enjoyed profound and far-reaching inspirations such as those of St Ignatius Loyola, St Teresa of Avila and St John of the Cross.

Indeed, theology struggled considerably, and only in the 19th and 20th centuries would it finally succeed in clarifying the main guidelines for its new overall direction, measured by its most important and lasting result with the Second Vatican Council.

But it is interesting to note that among the theologians who have been the object of more attentive meditation on the part of Jorge Mario Bergoglio, and now that he is Pope, also the object of explicit reference in his teaching, are some of the most lucid precursors and, in some cases, key players in this renewal. Among the first of these I am thinking of John Henry Newman, with his existential and dynamic concept of faith in contrast to a purely intellectual notion, and with his equally dynamic and historicized revival and illustration of the concept of tradition and the development of dogma, enriched by the enhancement of the dogmatic meaning of the *sensus fidei* of the people of God in contrast to an hierarchical view – to use Y. Congar's words – of the Church. But I am also thinking of Antonio Rosmini, who is much more influential than we might think in Pope Francis' thinking,[14] with his proposal, in his *Le cinque piaghe della santa Chiesa*[15] – so disconcertingly opportune – for reforming the Church in some of its crucial dimensions of life, and with his overall design for a Copernican revolution of how knowledge and cultural expression ought be structured. These are traced out with prophetic vigour and speculative rigour in his *Teosofia*.[16]

Yet, closer to us, in the 20th century, and in immediate preparation for the ecclesial event of epic significance which was Vatican II, is someone whom Pope Francis himself has recognized often for his positive and lasting influence in shaping his view of Christianity – Romano Guardini, whom some have not hesitated to call a 'Father of the twentieth century Church.' At the heart of the persevering and enormous commitment of this brilliant theologian and man

---

14 As Fulvio De Giorgi has shown in his *Quale ri-generazione della Chiesa nel rosminianesimo di papa Francesco?*, in F Bellelli – E Pili (eds.), *Ontologia, fenomenologia e nuovo umanesimo. Rosmini ri-generativo*, Città Nuova, Rome 2016, pp. 205-219.

15 A Rosmini, *Delle cinque piaghe della santa Chiesa*, Istituto di Studi Filosofici – Centro di Studi Rosminiani – Città Nuova Ed., Rome 1981. (The book has been published in English as *The Five Wounds of the Holy Church*, e.g. by HardPress Publishing, January 28, 2013, originally published in English in 1883 with an introduction by H.P. Liddon).

16 A Rosmini, *Teosofia*, Istituto di Studi Filosofici – Centro di Studi Rosminiani – Città Nuova Ed., 6 volumes, Rome 1998-2002. The entire work has not yet been translated into English.

of culture, there was the desire to help Christians in our day, especially the young, to 'see with new eyes', focusing on the methodical juncture of faith and the world, taking up faith not only in terms of its intellectual relevance in theology, but also its concrete cultural, artistic, anthropological, social relevance. It is no coincidence that many of the names that can be found among the most important mentions enriching the theological and cultural baggage of Pope Bergoglio can be found in the masterly studies that Guardini has put together and offered us, employing as his key to interpretation the positive and vital encounter between faith and culture that characterizes Christianity: Augustine, Bonaventure, Dante Alighieri, Pascal, Kierkegaard, Dostoevsky, Newman, Rilke ... Without exactly saying that it was Guardini who announced the work of the Council, back in 1922 he offered the prophetic and agenda-setting statement: 'A religious process of incalculable importance has begun – the Church is coming to life in souls,' a fact that has not only spiritual and religious consequences, but anthropological and social ones too, insofar as the Church, as Guardini writes, 'is for the individual, the living assumption of his personal perfection.'[17]

In this broad context, in which the best of the gospel as divulged and embodied in the light of the Holy Spirit becomes the principle of a logic capable of sustaining and promoting the relationship between personal identity and otherness, between communities, between peoples and

17 R GUARDINI, *Il senso della Chiesa (1922)*, Morcelliana, Brescia 2007. (The work exists in English as *The Meaning of the Church*, by Cluny Media, September 24, 2018).

cultures, one senses the weight that the principle of 'polar opposites' formulated by Guardini back in 1923[18] takes on in Pope Francis's view of things. Guardini is expressing a way of thinking, acting, managing things which is not based on Hegel's dialectic, in which the synthesis absorbs itself, destroying the parts in their identity and relational autonomy, identities that are in opposition to each other, but preserves them in a harmony in which each one can express itself by making room, through reciprocal recognition, for that more (the Ignatian '*magis*') that is released by and in their relationship. So it is not a dialectical ontology but a relational one, indeed a trinitarian one, to put it in terms used by Jean Danielou in 1968 in his little jewel of a work *La Trinité et le Mystère de l'Existence*.[19]

Hence Pope Francis' preferred image, the polyhedron. By contrast to the sphere, where every point is equidistant from the centre and there are no differences between one point and the other, the polyhedron is 'a geometric figure with many different facets' and thus 'reflects the confluence of all the partialities that in it keep their originality. Nothing is dissolved, nothing is destroyed, nothing is dominated, everything is integrated.'[20] This is a way of seeing and acting

18   In *Der Gegensatz. Versuche zu einer Philosophie des Lebendig-Konkreten*, Matthias Grünewald Verlag, Schöningh 1998.
19   Desclée de Brouwer, Paris 1968.
20   *Address to participants in the world meeting of popular movements*, Old Synod Hall, 28 October 2014; cf. *EG* 236: "Here our model is not the sphere, which is no greater than its parts, where every point is equidistant from the centre, and there are no differences between them. Instead, it is the polyhedron, which reflects the convergence of all its parts, each of which preserves its distinctiveness."

which we immediately understand to have very important consequences for how one looks at the Church and its mission, but also social and political life.

Other names can be mentioned as being among the theological sources for Pope Francis, names that are even closer to us. It is enough to think of three Jesuits who, though quite differently from one another, left a lasting imprint on the Church's journey in the second half of last century. In the first instance, Henri de Lubac, also a 'Father of the twentieth century Church' with his vision of the Church highlighting 'the social aspects of dogma' and forewarning against the ever-resurgent temptation to 'worldliness' (a recurring theme in Pope Francis' magisterium). But also Teilhard de Chardin, who, though he is somehow already there between the lines in *GS*, had long been ostracized by a whole strand of Catholic theology, and was then explicitly mentioned in a papal document for the first time, in Pope Francis' *LS*. Then finally, one we have already mentioned, Michel de Certeau. In his *The Mystical Fable*,[21] he re-interprets the ecclesial question within modernity with fervent passion and indomitable vigour, the question of the dynamic and fruitful shift of boundaries between theology, religion, mysticism, history and politics,[22] focusing on the

---

21 M DE CERTEAU, *La fable mystique* (XVIe-XVIIe siècle), Editions Gallimard, Paris 1982. Published in English as *The Mystical Fable*, Volume One, 'The Sixteenth and Seventeenth Centuries', University of Chicago Press, June 1995.

22 ID., *Politica e mistica. Questioni di storia religiosa*, Jaca Book, Milan 1975.

crucial question of the other[23] and the epic challenge of the foreigner as an appeal to finding harmony in difference.[24]

These are all topics and themes at the frontier where Pope Francis' magisterium abides and forcefully challenges us.

7. *Vatican II and Paul VI*

Someone has said that Pope Francis is the first 'postmodern' Pope. I believe this is basically true, if for no other reason than the fact that he seems so much at ease in the cultural climate we are going through, which is so multifaceted and elusive of any precise categorization, yet at the same time so challenging and promising. At ease: not in the sense that he agrees with it or wants to reach any compromise with it, let's be clear, but in the sense that he inhabits this cultural climate with the vigilant peace that comes from being in Christ, in the bosom of the Church, and at the service of promoting the Kingdom of God.

At any rate, one other thing is certain: that Pope Francis is the first Pope who did not take part in the Second Vatican Council. Yet conciliar teaching runs in his veins, enlightens his thinking, fires up his dreams, inspires his decisions. In other words, for him there is no conflict of interpretations … in his interpretation of the last Council. He said this himself, comprehensively, in the interview he gave Antonio

---

23 ID., *Mai senza l'altro. Viaggio nella differenza*, Edizioni Qiqajon, Magnano (BI) 1993.
24 ID., *L'Etranger ou union dans la différence*, Desclée de Brouwer, Paris 1969.

Spadaro in 2013, a few months after his election:

> Vatican II was a re-reading of the Gospel in light of contemporary culture. Vatican II produced a renewal movement that simply comes from the same Gospel. Its fruits are enormous ... Yes, there are hermeneutics of continuity and discontinuity, but one thing is clear: the dynamic of reading the Gospel, actualizing its message for today—which was typical of Vatican II—is absolutely irreversible.[25]

It couldn't be clearer than that! From a theological point of view one could say that Vatican II, in Pope Francis' eyes, is an updating of the message of Jesus offered to human history by the Church of Christ as it takes up the task of its mission in today's planetary and challenging context with creative fidelity and by listening to the Spirit. This is not the place for determining the extent to which the Council's magisterium has shaped Pope Francis' ministry or the orientation it has given such, not only because this has been done elsewhere, but also and especially because it is thoroughly embedded in everything about him (from his ecclesiological vision to the liturgy, from his concept of mission to his view of ecumenism, from inter-religious dialogue to how he sees the commitment of Christians to transformation of the world) as I will show briefly in the coming chapters. I think it is

---

25 A Spadaro, *Interview with Pope Francis*, http://w2.vatican.va/content/francesco/en/speeches/2013/september/documents/papa-francesco_20130921_intervista-spadaro.html

more useful, at this point in the journey, to indicate how the Council's creative reception has taken place in Jorge Mario Bergoglio, Jesuit, Bishop and now Pope, above all thanks to the mediation of two circumstances: on the one hand, post-conciliar papal magisterium, especially the magisterium of Paul VI, and on the other, the experience of the people of God in the Latin American Church, especially in Argentina.

Paul VI first of all. Especially now that we can interpret and evaluate Pope Montini's magisterium at some distance, and bearing in mind the history of its effects in practice (*Wirkungsgeschichte*), we see that he offered the broad directions within which to concretely channel, even initially, the interpretation of the Council and its reception in the conscience and practice of the people of God, It is no coincidence that the very title, *Evangelii Gaudium*, of Pope Francis' first and therefore agenda-setting Apostolic Exhortation, seems to want to grasp and revive the spirit that urged Pope Paul VI to write *Evangelii Nuntiandi* (8 December 1975) and *Gaudete in Domino* (9 May 1975). If the former is the most significant pastoral document in the panorama of post-conciliar magisterium – according to Pope Francis himself – this is so because by taking account of the situation and experiences of the people of God in the first decade after Vatican II, Paul VI, with penetrating evangelical discernment, saw the ways that the Church's mission was called by the Spirit to undertake in the manifold contexts of our time. And if the latter, *Gaudete in Domino*, seems just as significant for Pope Francis, it is because in it Paul VI, the 'modern' Pope so internally tormented by the drama of human beings and their history, reveals without shame what is the inner source and goal of human existence and the Church's mission: the joy of Christ which the world does not know and cannot give (cf. Jn 15:11).

This is Pope Francis' starting point: the joy of the gospel, where the genitive here is both subjective and objective, being both the joy which is the fruit of the gospel and the joy for which the gospel is what it is – an announcement of joy because it is an announcement of the measureless love of God for humanity and creation. These two words, joy and gospel, sum up Vatican II's message which focuses on the mystery of Christ not in and for itself, but precisely because it comes from the gospel and experiences the joy that comes from witnessing to the gospel and proclaiming it to everyone. This is the specific result of the updating (*aggiornamento*) that John XXIII had hoped from the Council and which Pope Paul VI, in the crucible of the trials experienced by the Council Assembly and then in the reception of its results, highlights as the guiding star for the Church's journey.

Yes, Paul VI: the Pope who chose the name of the Apostle to the Gentiles to express the new impetus for proclaiming the gospel that Vatican II was bringing about; the Pope who once again experienced like few others as a disciple of Christ and Pastor of the universal Church that the Gospel beatitudes are the Lord's promise to those who are poor, meek, pure of heart, builders of peace, to those who weep and are persecuted. This is where Pope Francis is starting out from. This is his wavelength, and he picks up two more great texts of Paul VI which the magisterium of both Pope John

Paul II and Benedict XVI further enriched: *Ecclesiam Suam* and *Populorum Progressio*. Two texts of capital importance.

Ecclesiam Suam, of a clarity that still surprises one, focuses on the three guidelines for updating on which the spiritual, theological, social movement experienced by Catholicism and, in general, by the whole Christian world in the twentieth century converge, and which the Council pursued with prophetic determination: the reawakening of the *awareness* the Church has of itself as creature and minister of Christ, the incarnate Word, who is its living heart through the power of the Holy Spirit; the *renewal* it is urgently called to so it can be more fully conformed to its Lord and Bridegroom; *dialogue* as the preferred way of carrying out its mission in the world today. Basically, the Church reform and concrete steps to it which Pope Francis' ministry appeals to and is so tenaciously and energetically committed to, head in this direction.

Then there is *Populorum Progressio*, the papal document which, perhaps more than any other in the post-conciliar period, quickened the practices of believers but also went beyond the confines of the Church to stir the consciences of the men and women of our day. It made one thing fully evident and tangible: that in the wake of the path inaugurated by Pope John XXIII's *Pacem in Terris*, the Church's mission is at the service of the universal promotion of justice, peace, solidarity and fraternity. The Church as 'teacher for humanity', handmaid of humanity, the Church – as Pope Francis says – which is 'poor and of the poor'. With *Populorum Progressio* the social magisterium of the Church clearly, and I would add irreversibly expressed the uniquely relevant gospel choice: that of being on the side of all of humanity, all human beings, which means, concretely, being on the side of those who live in the social and existential peripheries of the world or who are even marginalized and discarded by the world.

Pope Francis' *LS* picks this impetus up once more and breathes this prophetic spirit: enlightened by the gospel of Christ it jolts human consciousness, tears away the veil covering our eyes and makes us aware that the challenge of the planet's worldwide deterioration is doubly bound up with the challenge of poverty and waste, both of which challenge us to tackle, with courage and foresight, the crucial question of the change of cultural paradigm to the technocratic one which governs development in our society.

This requires a 'cultural revolution', as Pope Francis puts it, without beating around the bush.

8. *The road taken by the Church and theology in Latin America and Argentina, and the Aparecida Document*

Pope Francis has the clarity and courage to draw these things from the gospel, reinterpreted in the face of the challenges of today seen from the perspective of Vatican II not only because of the charism he enjoys as the Successor of Peter (though this is no small factor), but also because he has passionately experienced the troubled yet creative reception of the Council's message by the people of God in Latin America and, from what we have been told, has paid dearly for it in person. It is not a matter of making room for an exotic note with which to complete the picture of the spiritual, cultural and theological sources from which the magisterium of Pope Francis draws. It is something essential to it.

This is not the place, nor do I have the competence, to examine in any detail the substance and main developments that Latin American ecclesial and theological experience brought to the thinking and pastoral approach of the current Pope. Others have done this admirably: Juan Carlos Scannone, just to mention one, in his recent *La teología del pueblo. Raíces teológicas del papa Francesco*,[26] and I happily refer to works of this kind. It is enough to make this observation: the message of the Council, as a reinterpretation of the gospel mirrored in the challenges of today's world, found fertile ground for reception in the Latin American continent, undoubtedly due to the dramatic situation, the weight and urgency of the tasks the Church found itself, still finds itself, confronted with, but also because the reception process gave life to a grand movement involving every level of the people of God. It generated a Church phenomenon – if I may express it that way – that represents, even among the positives and negatives, the highs and lows and varied results, an effective testimony, so rich in promise, of the renewal put in place at the universal level by Vatican II. The election of a Latin American as Bishop of Rome and the first non-European pope makes the ecclesiological principle of catholicity especially evident, a principle expressed as

---

26 Editorial Sal Terrae, Maliaño (Cantabria) 2017.

follows in the Council's Constitution on the Church, *Lumen Gentium*:

> In virtue of this catholicity each individual part contributes through its special gifts to the good of the other parts and of the whole Church. Through the common sharing of gifts and through the common effort to attain fullness in unity, the whole and each of the parts receive increase. Not only, then, is the people of God made up of different peoples but in its inner structure also it is composed of various ranks (no. 13).

As we can see, we are talking about the logic of the polyhedron, an image so dear to Pope Francis because it expresses the profound dynamic of relationships in the universal Church, among local Churches, and in every local Church among its various components. At least two things can be highlighted in the text just quoted from *LG*: first of all the fact that every specific experience of Church, by virtue of the circumstances of inculturation of the gospel it has, expresses a unique face of the one Church and therefore bears its own peculiar gift with which to enrich all the others; secondly, the universal Church is a People, the People of God which lives among the peoples of the earth who are, each in their own way, an expression of the one People of God.

These are the two great guiding ideas which nurture the experience and understanding of the faith, in the light of Vatican II, of Pope Bergoglio, at the heart of the experience of Church in Latin America. On the one hand there is the way marked out, like so many milestones, by the General Assemblies of Bishops from the continent: from the first in Rio de Janeiro (1955) to those following in the wake of Vatican II at Medellín (1968), Puebla (1979), Santo Domingo (1992) and finally at Aparecida (2007), where the Archbishop of Buenos Aires, Bergoglio, was the President of the Drafting Commission for the final document which is known as the *Aparecida Document*. On the other hand, there is the experience of Church in Argentina where the theological current known as Liberation Theology had its own special emphasis. In various forms and with varying results, this current began with the famous book by Peruvian Gustavo Gutiérrez which laid out its program, *Teología de la liberación* (Liberation Theology),[27] a theology of the people (or by the people) and culture for whom Lucio Gera[28] was the inspiration and main exponent and which, because of its being strongly rooted in the ecclesial experience of the people of God, broke through the temptation to be taken over by the dialectical ideology of class struggle.

We could also say that the *Aparecida Document* is the successful and open meeting point for the promising developments of two directions that the Church in Latin America undertook in the years following the Council: one that involved the Church across the continent and one

27 *Teología de la liberación*, Centro de Estudios y Publicaciones, Lima 1971.
28 Cf. *Escritos Teológicas-Pastorales de Lucio Gera*, eds. V AZCUY, CM GALLI, M GONZÁLEZ, JB CAAMAÑO, 2 vols. Agápe-Facultad de Teología de la UCA, Buenos Aires 2006-2007.

that took root and sprouted especially in the Church in Argentina. One result of this and of the pastoral approach it expresses can be seen in the address given by Pope Francis in Rio de Janeiro on 28 July 2013 when he met with the bishops responsible for CELAM. He wanted to somehow express and relaunch the message of the Aparecida Conference in concrete pastoral terms. Let me emphasize three significant insights from this address.

a) The renewed appeal to '*the eyes of discipleship*' and '*the missionary disciple*' as the way to realize a hermeneutics for an evangelical interpretation of the socio-cultural situation of our day and of the Church's mission, not 'from outside' but 'from within' the gospel message and the Christian community: in order to thwart the danger of reverting to ideology and reductionism, in whatever form these may be present, and instead to be able to discern clearly and with relevance 'the steps that the Lord asks of us in the "today" of Latin America and the Caribbean', without retreating in sterile fashion into the past or embarking on utopian flights of fancy into the future.

b) The invitation to the *inner renewal* of the Church's life as a '*process*' of the people of God as a whole, and as a '*pastoral conversion*' that is actually effective because in the first instance it challenges attitudes and how people reform their lives, but also a '*pastoral discernment*' which clearly involves all components of ecclesial life, countering the risk of going back to clericalism. He also asked for an open and unprejudiced search for practical and worthwhile responses to people's existential issues, especially questions from the young.

c) The appeal to two pastoral categories in dialogue with society which copy 'the way God has revealed himself to us in history': *nearness and encounter*, because 'nearness takes the form of dialogue and creates a culture of encounter,' triggering the 'revolution of tenderness' which connotes an anthropological experience of God's becoming man in the flesh of Christ.

Well then, these pastoral indications, determined by Aparecida's choice of 'mission as paradigm', are committed to expressing the historical vitality of the trinitarian principle of the virtuous circle between God and humanity in Christ which is the mature result of Vatican II's Christian consciousness. They suggest and indeed demonstrate how spirituality, theology, pastoral ministry, culture, and social involvement belong to the Church's mission and are enriched by it. It bears witness to the peculiar and original contribution that the Latin American Church, in its pastoral practice and its theology, offers the whole Church when the message of the Second Vatican Council is embodied this way: both from the point of view of the *social question* in the all-important anthropological, social and ecological terms in which it is posed today, and in terms of the *pedagogical and pastoral strategy* to be thought out and implemented in order to develop the kind of awareness and behaviours that come from this approach.

Chapter 3
SPEAKING OF GOD TODAY AS HE SPEAKS THROUGH THE GOSPEL OF JESUS

1. Reform thinking

Pope Francis writes as follows in *Laudato Si'*:

> We need to develop a new synthesis capable of overcoming the false arguments of recent centuries. Christianity, in fidelity to its own identity and the rich deposit of truth which it has received from Jesus Christ, continues to reflect on these issues in fruitful dialogue with changing historical situations. In doing so, it reveals its eternal newness (no. 121).

After reviewing, in the previous chapters, some of the main sources for the experience and understanding of the faith which inspire Pope Francis' ministry, in this chapter and the two brief ones that come after it I would like to highlight how these sources are at work in his efforts to re-express the gospel in dialogue with the circumstances of history and the epic changes of our day.[1]

---

1 Cf. contributions contained in K Appel – J Helmut Deible (Eds.), *Barmherzigkeit und zärtliche Liebe. Das theologische Programm von Papst Franziskus*, Verlag Herder, Freiburg im Breisgau 2016.

I am taking my cue in this chapter from the obviously central challenge: how we feel, think about and then speak about God.² Some time ago, a friend told me about a comment by a bishop who carries out an important role in the service of the universal Church: 'That such and such a theologian' he said 'still speaks about God ... that's not just rare today, it is unique!' Perhaps it was an overly severe assessment, but it does picture a situation in which theology, and more broadly, the culture of Christian inspiration, struggles more than a bit to find the right words for communicating the freshness and joy of God that Jesus Christ touches hearts and minds with.

Theology is not alone in this. The fact is, that as Edgar Morin puts it, the real challenge of our time is none other than to 'reform thinking'.³ In this indecisive, fluid and troubled dawning of post-modernity, it is a question of rethinking the form, style and rhythm of the way we have thought and interpreted things in practice. Now, while it is true that our thinking about God as it comes from the gospel of Jesus has kept its critical distance and preserved truth and meaning which is different from dominant mainstream thinking, it is just as true that it has felt the repercussions of the latter and suffered its temptations. The challenge to 'reform thinking' is an invitation, then, and an opportunity for thinking that

2 Cf. A Cozzi – R Repole – G Piano, *Papa Francesco. Quale teologia?*, Cittadella, Assisi 2016.
3 Cf. E Morin, *La tête bien faite*, Seuil 1999; It. tr., *La testa ben fatta. Riforma dell'insegnamento e riforma del pensiero*, Raffaello Cortina Editore, Milan 2000.

feeds on the gospel and is called to measure itself by the face of God as proclaimed by the gospel.

In other words, how we feel, think about and speak of God in a new way is not a need coming only from the socio-cultural context but comes from the very core of faith itself. Of course it is true, therefore, that the new stage of evangelization that the Church is called to is the reason urging us to rediscover the joy of encounter with God, the God of Jesus, so we can proclaim it and bear witness to it in a way that is relevant, coherent and telling; but this reason is intrinsic to the gospel itself, since how we feel and think about God is the criteria for and the verification of evangelization, of a life that qualifies as the life led by missionary disciples.

Who can the Church bear witness to and proclaim if not the face of the God of Jesus, since it is He whom it has encountered and by whom it has been transfigured?

2. *The encounter with Jesus Christ as principle and measure*

Yet, what does it mean, or better still, what does it imply to rethink God according to the logic of the gospel of Jesus?

It implies, first of all, as a condition and way of being relevant, being open to God to welcome him into our thinking and then to communicate him in words and gestures which suit him: a suitability not measured by human suitability but by who he is in himself. And already – in direct contact with the thought that pulsates in *Evangelii Gaudium* (*EG*) – the fact that we can and should make such a statement is of decisive importance. It means that we are taking the singular event that determines how we speak of God in Jesus Christ seriously: going beyond any abstract dialectic between overwhelming theocentrism and presumed anthropocentrism.

No! The place for talking about God is Jesus Christ, and it is the encounter with him which is the point of departure and the horizon for thinking about God in ways that are suitable to God within human existence. 'Being a Christian is not the result of an ethical choice or a lofty idea, but the encounter with an event, a person, which gives life a new horizon and a decisive direction' (*EG*, no. 7), says Pope Francis, recalling Pope Benedict's words with gratitude.[4]

This implies a grace and a responsibility: letting our thinking about God be shaped by and in Christ's thinking, while being attentive to the breath of his Spirit. As the Apostle Paul teaches: 'For what person knows a man's thoughts except the spirit of the man which is in him? So also no one comprehends the thoughts of God except the Spirit of God. Now we have received not the spirit of the world, but the Spirit which is from God, that we might understand the gifts bestowed on us by God ... we have the mind (*noûs*) of Christ' (1 Cor 2:11-12, 16b).

This is the key that Pope Francis strikes so often: he does so, for example, in no. 94 of *EG*, and returns to it in the address he gave to the National Convention of the Italian Church in Italy, at Florence in November 2015. He tells them that it is about freeing our thinking about God from

---

[4] Cf. BENEDICT XVI, Encyclical *Deus Caritas Est*, 25 December 2005, no. 1.

its tendency to Pelagiansim and Gnosticism, 'manifestations of anthropocentric immanentism' where the faith dissolves because they 'ultimately keep one imprisoned in his or her own thoughts and feelings' (*EG* 94).

The diagnosis is fitting: thinking about God is contradictory, misguided and even blasphemous if it pretends to capture God within narrow individual thinking. The *ratio Dei* draws its truth from being fed by the *oratio coram Deo* and when it is immersed in *adoratio* of his mystery:[5] that is, when it passes from a *fassendes Denken* to a *lassendes Denken*, from a grasping way of thinking to a hospitable way of thinking,[6] when it does not yield to the illusion of being final and perfect but sees itself as being open, incomplete, restless.[7]

This happens when 'thanks solely to this encounter – or renewed encounter – with God's love, which blossoms into an enriching friendship, we are liberated from our narrowness and self-absorption' so that ' we become fully human when we become more than human, when we let God bring us beyond ourselves in order to attain the fullest truth of our being' (*EG*, 8). But for it to happen we have to surmount two temptations.

---

5 Cf. M Cacciari, *Il pregio dell'ascolto*, in *Martini e noi*, ed. M. Vergottini, Ed. Piemme, Milan 2015, pp. 36-37.

6 The expression comes from K Hemmerle, *Das Heilige und das Denken. Zur philosophischen Phänomenologie des Heiligen*, in Id., *Auf den göttlichen Gott zudenken (Ausgewählte Schriften*, Band 1), Herder, Freigburg-Basel-Wien 1996, pp. 111-117.

7 Cf. Pope Francis, *Homily in the Church of the Gesù*, 3 January 2014.

The first is always the resurgence of *thinking about God from the outside, compared to his being present*, as if thinking and speaking about God were ultimately something done from without rather than encountering and knowing God in Jesus, that is, speaking of our experience of him in an act of faith and love which comes from believing in him.

No! Thinking and speaking about God as the gospel does are things that take place in the act of faith and love with which I give myself to him because I have encountered him and am drawn to him. This means that thinking and speaking about God involve not only the mind but the heart, not only an exercise of knowledge but also the experience of wisdom, since he is not only the word (*lógos*) but also 'spirit and life' (*pneûma* and *zoe*). This does not mean ignoring the demands of reason, but transfiguring reason and constantly immersing it in the depths of Christ's Pasch, his death and resurrection. Ultimately, the 'temptation is to shift reason away from where God our Father placed it. It was given to us to throw light on faith.'[8]

Hence a second temptation: that of *thinking from the outside compared to God's being present in our relationship with others and with history, in Jesus*. It is not really God that is being thought of – not the God of Jesus Christ, Emmanuel, God-with-us – when he is thought about in ways that fall short of his presence and activity in the very act with which I address the other, communicate with the other, walk with the other and make history with the other. Thinking about God,

---

8 J BERGOGLIO (Pope Francis), *Nel cuore di ogni padre. Alle radici della sua spiritualità*, Bur Rizzoli, Milan 2014, p. 163.

the God of Jesus Christ, is an act of relationship in itself and brings about relationship. It is effective and performative.

> This principle has to do with incarnation of the word and its being put into practice: ... The principle of reality, of a word already made flesh and constantly striving to take flesh anew, is essential to evangelization ... it impels us to put the word into practice, to perform works of justice and charity which make that word fruitful. Not to put the word into practice, not to make it reality, is to build on sand, to remain in the realm of pure ideas and to end up in a lifeless and unfruitful self-centredness and gnosticism (*EG* 233).

3. At the heart of the kerygma with a new language

Overcoming these two temptations of thinking externally about God and offering that to others, compared to the God Jesus Christ brings us into relationship with, leads to two tasks that Pope Francis asks us to honour courageously and energetically.

The first is to go to the heart of the Christian *kerygma* and take our cue from there alone: 'Where your synthesis is, there lies your heart,' says Francis in one of his well-chosen slogans (*EG*, 143).[9] We often find attempts to formulate

---

9   The principle which, according to Pope Francis, we should be inspired by, along the lines of, for example, the principle which held sway during the drafting of the *Catechism of the Catholic Church*,

this synthesis in his magisterium. I am thinking of no. 4 of *EG* where we read: 'God with his people in the midst of a celebration overflowing with the joy of salvation ... "The Lord, your God is in your midst, a warrior who gives you the victory; he will rejoice over you with gladness, he will renew you in his love; he will exult over you with loud singing, as on a day of festival" (Zeph 3:17).' Or no. 128 where he proposes the 'fundamental announcement' of the gospel in these terms: 'the personal love of God who became man, who gave himself up for us, who is living and who offers us his salvation and his friendship.' Or again in no. 164, where he says that the 'kerygma, which needs to be the centre of all evangelizing activity and all efforts at Church renewal' is 'trinitarian': 'The fire of the Spirit is given in the form of tongues and leads us to believe in Jesus Christ who, by his death and resurrection, reveals and communicates to us the Father's infinite mercy.'

Each of these 'brief formulas'[10] deserves careful analysis. But it is enough to at least note some of their characteristic features. First of all, the centrality of mercy, insofar as it is the heart of God who reveals himself in order to accept, heal and transfigure human history. Hence its essential

that is, the principle of the 'hierarchy of truths' formulated by Vatican II in its Decree *Unitatis Redintegratio*: "When comparing doctrines with one another, they should remember that in Catholic doctrine there exists a "hierarchy" of truths, since they vary in their relation to the fundamental Christian faith" (no. 11).

10   The expression comes from K Rahner, *Per una «formula breve» della fede cristiana*, in *Nuovi saggi* III, Edizioni Paoline, Rome 1969, pp. 175-189; Id., *Problemi su una formula breve di fede*, in *Nuovi Saggi* IV, edizioni Paoline, Rome 1973, pp. 313-352.

mystagogical connotation (cf. *EG* 166), the introduction into the mystery of God and accompanying people as they enter and stay there, since 'each person's situation before God and their life in grace are mysteries which no one can fully know from without' (no. 172). Also the other essential community and social connotation, since 'The content of the first proclamation has an immediate moral implication centred on charity' (no. 177). This not only means reaffirming the socially performative nature of the knowledge of God transmitted by the *kerygma*, but also recalling the need to develop – as Paul VI writes in *Evangelii Nuntiandi* (*EN*), 43 – a 'spiritual sensitivity for reading God's message in events' (*EG* 154), and carefully discerning 'a call which God causes to resound in the historical situation itself. In this situation, and also through it, God calls the believer' (*ivi*).[11]

The second task to honour concerns the style and formulation with which the proclamation of the God of Jesus Christ is made.

> The centrality of the kerygma calls for stressing those elements which are most needed today: it has to express God's saving love which precedes any moral and religious obligation on our part; it should not impose the truth but appeal to freedom; it should be marked by joy, encouragement, liveliness and a harmonious balance which will not reduce preaching to a few doctrines which are at times more philosophical

---

11   A statement made by John Paul II in his post-synodal Apostolic Exhortation *Pastores Dabo Vobis*, 25 March 1992, no. 10.

than evangelical. All this demands on the
part of the evangelizer certain attitudes which
foster openness to the message: approachability,
readiness for dialogue, patience, a warmth and
welcome which is non-judgemental (EG 165).

Hence the reminder of the hermeneutical criterion spelt out by John XXIII in his address at the opening of Vatican II, which does not fail to spur us on as a benefit and providential thorn in the flesh as we rethink how we think and speak about God: 'The deposit of faith is one thing; the way it is expressed is another' (*EG* 41).[12]

Two notes on this are sufficient. The first: Pope Francis invites us to give careful thought to 'constantly seek ways of expressing unchanging truths in a language which brings out their abiding newness' (*EG* 41). This does not only mean, put negatively, that we run the serious risk of holding fast to a formulation of doctrine without conveying the substance (cf. *ivi*) but also, expressed positively, that doctrinal formulation is in itself intended to transmit the interpersonal relationship in the *hic et nunc* of the event which is the encounter with the merciful and liberating truth of God in Christ. Pope Francis notes that 'conceptual tools exist to heighten contact with the realities they seek to explain, not to distance us from

---

12   Cf. JOHN XXIII, *Address at the solemn opening of Vatican Council II* (11 October 1962): *AAS* 54 (1962), 786: "Est enim aliud ipsum depositum fidei, seu veritates, quae veneranda doctrina nostra continentur, aliud modus, quo eaedem enuntiatur (One thing is the deposit of faith or truths contained in our venerable doctrine, and another thing is the way in which they are announced, always however with the same meaning and acceptance)."

them' (*EG* 194). It is not only an insistence on the realism of faith,[13] but of opening the eyes of the heart to the living encounter with the eyes of Christ which happens through the work of the Holy Spirit.

St John of the Cross, the Doctor of faith, teaches us this in his *Spiritual Canticle* where he calls the doctrinal truths proposed by faith 'silvered surfaces', while what they contain and pass on is compared to 'gold'.[14] The truths transmitted by faith, covered in the silver of doctrine, refer to the gold of their substance – God himself.

Now – and it is this that the human being yearns for, argues John of the Cross – if only these silver-covered truths at a certain point suddenly, to our great amazement, might become the place of encounter with eyes to see with that we desire with all our being! When that happens, the surprise is that the desire to contemplate those eyes reveals its secret: to be looked at by those eyes in turn, and in the first instance, with tenderness and love.

This is the knowledge of God that the New Testament describes as knowing 'face to face' (cf. 1 Cor 13:12; 1 Jn 3:2). It is the shift from doctrinal knowledge which simply represents the reality, to an existential knowledge which takes place between persons: eyes in eyes. With this idea we can briefly describe three guidelines that Pope Francis'

---

13   Cf. Thomas Aquinas, S. Th., II-II, q. 1, a. 2, ad 2: "Actus fidei non terminatur ad enuntiabile, sed ad rem (The believer's act of faith does not terminate in the propositions, but in the realities which they express).

14   Cf. JOHN OF THE CROSS, *Spiritual Canticle*, verses 11 and 12.

magisterium offers us to follow in order to reach this objective.

4. Flesh and mystery

Here are two of the key words of his magisterium: because it is through the flesh of Christ, extended in the flesh of his brothers and sisters, that we encounter the mystery of God and can open ourselves to him, welcome him, become friends, communicate him. God is not encountered 'without flesh and without the cross' says Pope Francis, and he explains:

> The Gospel tells us constantly to run the risk of a face-to-face encounter with others, with their physical presence which challenges us, with their pain and their pleas, with their joy which infects us in our close and continuous interaction. True faith in the incarnate Son of God is inseparable from self-giving, from membership in the community, from service, from reconciliation with others. The Son of God, by becoming flesh, summoned us to the revolution of tenderness (*EG* 88).

This is not simply a figure of speech but an effective presentation of the *ontology of grace which flourishes in the ethos of charity*. Yes, because through the incarnation of the Word of God by the breath of the Spirit we become sharers in the mystery of God himself. It means he is *interior intimo meo* ('more inward to me than my most inward part') and at the same time *superior summo meo* ('higher than my highest') to put it in Augustine's words.[15] But conversely, it is something by which the human being, each of us, becomes in a certain sense an intimate friend of God's: 'To believe that the Son of God assumed our human flesh means that each human person has been taken up into the very heart of God' says Francis (*EG* 178).

Human flesh, through Christ, taken into the heart of God: this is the ontology of grace. 'Every human being is the object of God's infinite tenderness, and he himself is present in their lives' (*EG* 274), thus making us again and again the privileged object of his tenderness: this is the gospel ethos of love for our brothers and sisters.

We find an essential way forward here for the way we feel, think about and speak of the mystery of God who reveals himself in the history of humankind in Jesus. We know how an essential gain came about in Christian self-consciousness with Francis of Assisi, Ignatius of Loyola, Teresa of Avila, and how it was eventually shaped at the level of spirituality and praxis: the gain was discovering the flesh of Christ as the only way to participate in the mystery of God, the Trinity.

In harmony with this spiritual tradition, with the teaching of Vatican II in *Gaudium et Spes* (cf. no 22: 'For by His incarnation the Son of God has united Himself in some fashion with every man') and John Paul II in *Redemptor Hominis* (man 'the way of the Church'), Pope Francis goes a step further and says:

---

15   AUGUSTINE, *Confessions*, Part 3, Ch. 6,11.

> God's word teaches that our brothers and sisters are the prolongation of the incarnation for each of us: "As you did it to one of these, the least of my brethren, you did it to me" (Mt 25:40). The way we treat others has a transcendent dimension: "The measure you give will be the measure you get" (Mt 7:2). It corresponds to the mercy which God has shown us: "Be merciful, just as your Father is merciful" (Lk 6:36) (*EG* 179).

What does it all imply for how we feel, think about and speak of God? It implies not only learning from God, in Christ, the right gaze and attitude regarding one another, but being responsibly and creatively involved in facing the other as the one to whom he has united himself in Christ and communicates himself in the Spirit.

In a word, it means learning 'to remove our sandals before the sacred ground of the other' as Pope Francis writes in *EG* 169, with a reference that should not surprise us: Ex 3:5. It echoes God's word to Moses: 'Remove your sandals because the place where you are standing is holy ground!' So it is God we are talking about. But God has become flesh in Christ and the flesh of Christ is extended in the flesh of every human being. So then …

Starting from this Christ-centred (and trinitarian) ontology we can see the ethical outlook guiding Francis in the matter of accompanying the journey of marriage and the family (see *Amoris Laetitia*) as well as his other clear positions in the area of social teaching: 'Ethics' he writes, referring to the economy 'leads to a God who calls for a committed response which is outside the categories of the marketplace. When these latter are absolutized, God can only be seen as uncontrollable, unmanageable, even dangerous, since he calls human beings to their full realization and to freedom from all forms of enslavement' (*EG* 57).

It is the relationship with God in Christ, ultimately, rethinking things in communion with *this* God, starting out from the gospel, that guides the Christian ethos at a personal and social level. What is essential is that every action and project bears 'the mark of Christ incarnate, crucified and risen' (*EG* 95).

5. *Time as kairos and process*

For Pope Francis, who quotes Peter Faber in this regard, 'time is God's messenger' (*EG* 171). So much so that rethinking God means contemplating and experiencing the mystery of time through which God announces himself and makes himself present in Jesus Christ.

On close scrutiny, we see a plainly evangelical sacramental notion of time, critical of 'pastoral acedia' (*EG* 82) and 'the gray pragmatism of the daily life of the Church' (*EG* 83), coming from wanting to 'dominate the rhythm of life', excluding access to the surprise at God's breaking into our lives when he visits us and the patient accompanying presence with which he takes care of us. The God of Jesus is the God whose messenger is time: in the *kairos* of his irruption into our lives which invites us to encounter and challenges our decisions; and in the *process* which looks to the 'horizon of the utopian future' and 'fullness' as 'the final cause which draws us to itself' (no. 222).

Even before being a criterion for pastorally effective action, this healthy experience and concept of time is the acknowledgement of true thinking about God according to the logic of the gospel, which announces the *kairós* of the coming of the Kingdom (cf. Mk 1:14-15) and the immediacy of the encounter with salvation, while also inviting us to trust in and be patient with the seed that will bear fruit only in due time and to varying degrees (cf. Mk 4:3-9; 26-29) and which even pays the worker who arrived at the last moment with unheard of generosity according to human rules for that sort of thing (cf. Mt 20:1-16).

The spiritual and theological concept of time as a sacrament of the coming of the Kingdom of God in history, becomes, then, the demanding criterion and verification of how we rethink God and his action in our lives as 'missionary disciples'.

Hence there are a number of pastoral principles which come back as a leitmotiv in the magisterium of Pope Francis' words and gestures: Giving priority to time means being concerned about *initiating processes rather than possessing spaces*' which means giving 'priority to actions which generate new processes in society and engage other persons and groups who can develop them' (*EG* 223); personal accompaniment of growth processes (nos 169 ff.); with trust, once again in God, that 'true Christian hope, which seeks the eschatological kingdom, always generates history' (no. 181).

6. *Harmonizing differences*

Rethinking the God of Jesus, the Father, Son and Holy Spirit, finally urges us to rethink the paradigm of unity and multiplicity, of identity and dialogue, of self-expression and friendship with others. Theological literature on the Trinity in recent decades has offered us abundant material for reflection on this.

The unity we are talking about in contemplating the mystery of the God of Jesus is not monolithic or a unity of uniformity. But seeing the value of diversity should not take us in the direction of relativism, the disintegration of truth. In this context Pope Francis offer two important indications for moving forward.

It is no coincidence – here is the first, which we have already had the opportunity to spend time with, recalling the lesson of St Basil – that he insists on the specific and indispensable role of the Holy Spirit, and therefore of vigilant and active obedience to his actions, in the event of the free convergence in Christ of the relationships we experience: He is the guarantor and promoter of creative freedom and the process of living together in convivial ways. 'The Holy Spirit, sent by the Father and the Son, transforms our hearts and enables us to enter into the perfect communion of the blessed Trinity, where all things find their unity' (*EG* 117) Pope Francis notes. And again: 'Diversity must always be reconciled by the help of the Holy Spirit; he alone can raise up diversity, plurality and multiplicity while at the same time bringing about unity' (no. 131).

Hence the second guideline: the free and mysterious action of the Spirit, which always transcends our thinking, our expectations, our plans, takes on the flesh of the actions and dramas of history, working 'to face conflict head on, to resolve it and to make it a link in the chain of a new process' (*EG* 227). The action of the Spirit, in fact, passes through the contradiction of the cross, takes it up and opens it up to the logic of encounter, reconciliation, exchange of gifts.

From the face of God which challenges us in the crucified Lord who gives us the Holy Spirit 'without measure' (cf. Jn 3:34), comes 'a way of making history in a life setting where conflicts, tensions and oppositions can achieve a diversified and life-giving unity. This is not to opt for a kind of syncretism, or for the absorption of one into the other, but rather for a resolution which takes place on a higher plane and preserves what is valid and useful on both sides' (*EG* 228).

Chapter 4
JOYFULLY FOLLOWING THE GOSPEL TO 'BRING NEW RELATIONSHIPS' INTO THE WORLD

1. With the Easter Christ at the heart of the world

Pope Francis' words in the second chapter of *Evangelii Gaudium* (EG) can only but command our attention as he speaks of 'new relationships brought by Christ' (cf. nos 87-92). Thus he projects our gaze toward the fiery centre of history and the cosmos: the Easter Christ. More than a projection it is an urging – to immerse mind and heart in this living centre and re-emerge renewed, at the side of the poor, the excluded and the discarded members of society and as both witnesses to and actors in the proclamation of the new world that the gospel gives birth to each day:

> Christ's resurrection is not an event of the past; it contains a vital power which has permeated this world. Where all seems to be dead, signs of the resurrection suddenly spring up. It is an irresistible force ... Each day in our world beauty is born anew, it rises transformed through the storms of history. Values always tend to reappear under new guises, and human beings have arisen time after time from situations that seemed doomed. Such is the power of the resurrection,

and all who evangelize are instruments of that power (*EG* 276).

Jesus the Christ is crucified today in the crosses of humanity, and rises again today at the heart of the world. Rays of new life radiate from him, from the Spirit poured out 'without measure (cf. Jn 3:34) on all flesh (cf. Acts 2:17). This is the vision of the new humanity in Christ which Pope Francis presents through his ministry. It goes even further: he presents the amazing and grateful experience of Christogenesis which has permeated the world, transforming from within and below the abyss of human tragedies, the most purulent and infected wounds of human affairs.

This faith and hope transform Pope Francis' outlook on the world into light and tenderness. This is the anthropology that springs from the gospel, from the Church's tradition, from Vatican II. He lives it and he proclaims it. The 'new stage of evangelization' he urges the Church to take is nothing else but 'the power of the resurrection,' and 'all who evangelize are instruments of that power' (*EG* 276).

There is no doubt that we can recognize the emphases and spirit of Vatican II in all this. But there is something more. The message Pope Francis addresses to us is like a lens focusing the sun's rays, causing the flame to ignite and flare up. The lesson of Vatican II, as focused and assimilated by Pope Francis in the crucible of the Church's journey following the Council, becomes a principle for life in the Church's journey and consciousness. It triggers the 'revolution of tenderness' he wants every dimension of life and every expression of the mission of the Church as it 'goes forth' to be clothed in. This is how the Pope feels and the *sensus fidei* of the people of God is spontaneously and very closely in correspondence with this.

'*Yes*' then, '*to the new relationships brought by Christ.*'

2. Mediating the 'new creation'

The fundamental issue here is that the solution 'will never be found in fleeing from a personal and committed relationship with God which at the same time commits us to serving others' (*EG 91*). Commitment (com = with) implies personal relationship. Pledging, exposing, offering oneself only happens in interpersonal relationship: 'it means learning to find Jesus in the faces of others, in their voices, in their pleas' (*EG 91*).

The personal relationship which decides on 'community commitment' in the Church and for the world, passes through Jesus. It comes from him and in him in and through personal relationships. This is neither a simple point of departure nor a final point of arrival. It is an event. It happens every time we go forth from ourselves and pledge ourselves to God by pledging ourselves to our neighbour.

We might think this is something we can already take for granted, but it is not the case. This concrete experience of the resurrection of Jesus still has to become the breath and style of daily life: and if it does, it is a gift, like a seed full of novelty and in expectation of the coming of the Kingdom hidden in the heart of every human being. It all hangs on personal relationships. It is in and through personal relationships that God's gaze becomes our gaze in Christ.

Simone Weil writes:

> The real aim is not to see God in all things; it is that God through us should see the things that we see. God has got to be on the side of the subject and not on that of the object during all those intervals of time when, forsaking the contemplation of the light, we imitate the descending movement of God so as to turn ourselves toward the world. We must not go to the help of our neighbour for Christ, but through Christ. Let the 'I' disappear in such a way that Christ, thanks to the intermediary formed by our soul and body, himself goes to the help of our neighbour.[1]

EG traces out three grand trajectories for this experience in our lives: reconciliation with the flesh of others (cf. no. 88), opening our hearts wide (cf. no. 272), the sense of mystery (cf. no. 279). It is about revealing the rhythm and meaning of what happens when there are 'new relationships brought by Christ' in an ongoing act of community discernment which becomes a mediation of the new creation which the resurrection of Jesus gives birth to from deep within the world.

3. *Flesh is God's way*

Francis adds to the Church's lexicon, at least the one in operation in recent centuries, through his constant

---

1 S Weil, Notebooks, 2, Routledge and Kegan Paul 1956, p. 358.

reference to the 'flesh'. The fact is that the experience and understanding of the Christian faith has sinned with regard to the flesh through its indifference and suspicion of it, and perhaps even through ignoring and removing it. The *metánoia* given and requested of us by the gospel has so far only gone a certain way in its long journey through hearts and minds. It has not yet become a culture through and through, meaning it has not become a lifestyle and way of thinking.

A significant direction in research carried out by philosophy, the human and natural sciences today actually opens up and explores a new path to our way of thinking and feeling. We perceive – as Maurice Merleau-Ponty writes, for example – that the flesh envelops us, expressing the being that we are and in which we are, insofar as it is the real condition of possibility for the communication in which the relationship of self with itself, with others, with the world takes place. So much so that the sense of being is only given to us in the all-engrossing drama of the flesh, and looks upon it from the ambiguous (that is, undecided, and as such to be decided in freedom) threshold of the ever new encounter between the 'I' and the Other in the world but also beyond it, in an inexhaustible play of access to transcendence which actually comes from immanence itself.[2]

The experience and understanding of discipleship of Jesus

---

2 Cf. M FOGARTY *Corpo e mondo in Maurice Merleau-Ponty. La carne e il suo senso tra unità e ambiguità*, Istituto Universitario Sophia, Figline e Incisa Valdarno (Florence) 2015, still in process of publication.

have a very special talent here to make use of for acquiring and transfiguring this approach. Flesh is God's way. Is not Christian faith focused on a *Logos* who 'became flesh' (Jn 1:14)? And did it not get to the point where Tertullian said that '*caro cardo salutis est*'?[3] We are asked to take the risk, have the courage, the simplicity of pursuing this way ourselves, the way of flesh. Deep down, without stopping too soon out of timidity or false prudence.

This implies, first of all, redefining the relationship between male and female, the first of the 'new relationships brought by Jesus.' The imbalance in ecclesial understanding and practice nowadays is so pronounced as to be intolerable. Only in relationship of one's own flesh with the flesh of others can we go the way of healing this rupture between soul and body, spirit and flesh, affection and reason.

But this means looking at things more broadly, taking hold of the discernment process regarding technology and how it predisposes things to extend human flesh in reference to self and looking after our 'common home'. Following the trajectory of 'reconciliation with the flesh' we begin to understand the importance of the 'integral ecology' spoken about in *Laudato Si* (*LS*).

The crucial contribution of the gospel in overcoming the dominant paradigm – androcentric on the one hand and technocratic on the other – can neither be benefited from nor become effective without radically rethinking the interpretative model of 'natural law', conceived of in abstract

---

3   Cf. *De resurrectione mortuorum*, VIII, 6-7.

terms irrespective of the historical consciousness offered us by Revelation. Certain approaches to theology still persist in dealing this way with questions relating to anthropology and sexuality, ecology and technology.

4. *Hearts opened wide*

In this case too, the expression is poignant and provocative. It calls us to our inner depths as the place in which heart and mind are immersed in God: but at the same time it invites us to extend our boundaries and discover distant horizons, extend hospitality.

The expression 'hearts opened wide' aims at expressing a specific aspect of our inner self: the evangelical aspect wrought by the coming of the Kingdom and the resurrection of Jesus. Here is how Pope Francis describes it:

> When we live out a spirituality of drawing nearer to others and seeking their welfare, our hearts are opened wide to the Lord's greatest and most beautiful gifts. Whenever we encounter another person in love, we learn something new about God (EG 272).

What captures our attention is the reference to spirituality which is not just an inwardly-focused individual exercise but as an experience of 'us' brought about by the Risen Christ in the encounter of self with others.[4] This

---

4 Cf. JC SCANNONE, *Il soggetto comunitario della spiritualità della mistica popolari*, in "La Civiltà Cattolica", no. 3950 (17 January 2015), pp. 126-141.

concept of spirituality [in the Italian original of *GS* it is '*la mistica*'], an important semantic shift by comparison with its usual meaning, is relevantly re-positioned within the context of Jesus' gospel.

In fact, it designates the place where relationship with God occurs – and without ceasing to be such it is intensified by the way it communicates – through relationship in Jesus *with others in the world*. This is how our inner being, [represented by heart in the English translation of *GS*], is 'opened wide' to others and is experienced as a place of encounter with God and, in him, with one and all. The 'interior castle' – without lessening its quality of inwardness but rather enhancing it – is thus extended to becoming the 'exterior castle'.[5] God, who in Jesus dwells in me, through the Spirit, also dwells where two or more are gathered in his Name (cf. Mt 18:20), in the encounter with the other as an experience of 'mystical fraternity' (*EG* 92). Mysticism, therefore, without a doubt: as a personal experience of union with God in Christ, but of God where he came in Christ and comes today – in the other's flesh. A very important consequence results: '*The realism of the social aspect of the*

---

5 The link between the 'interior castle' which St Teresa of Avila talks about, and the 'exterior castle' which designates the presence of Christ among human beings, comes from a present-day mystic, Chiara Lubich: cf. JC CERVERA OCD, *Il castello esteriore – il "nuovo" nella spiritualità di Chiara Lubich*, ed. F. Ciardi, Città Nuova, Rome 2011; and the Proceedings of the theological seminar at the Istituto Universitario Sophia (12-13 June 2014) published in A CLEMENZA – V DI PLATO – J TREMBLAY (Eds.), *Castello interiore e Castello esteriore. Per una grammatica dell'esperienza cristiana*, Città Ideale, Prato 2015.

Gospel (*EG* 88):

> To believe that the Holy Spirit is at work in everyone means realizing that he seeks to penetrate every human situation and all social bonds ... Evangelization is meant to cooperate with this liberating work of the Spirit. The very mystery of the Trinity reminds us that we have been created in the image of that divine communion, and so we cannot achieve fulfilment or salvation purely by our own efforts. From the heart of the Gospel we see the profound connection between evangelization and human advancement, which must necessarily find expression and develop in every work of evangelization (EG 178).

Mystical experience of the truly divine God as he reveals himself in Jesus does not tear us away from history to drown the self in the always indefinable indefinite: but it is the sap that makes the blood of God flow in the flesh of the world. Government by *oíkos* and *pólis*, the economy and politics, and looking after our common home, science and technology – these are not affairs which are outside the coming of the Kingdom. They must remain autonomous, but this autonomy instead is the place and vehicle for the realization of human history and the cosmos.

The social alternative of the gospel takes shape among the opposing temptations of the *fuga mundi* and theocratic *christianitas*: leaven, salt, light that give shape and taste and orientation to the events of the world. The commandment to love one another is in fact 'Heaven's praxis',[6] and it becomes the same on earth. Hence the fundamental pillars of the teaching of Pope Francis in terms of the continuous updating of the Church's social doctrine in dialogue with current challenges:

> the intimate relationship between the poor and the fragility of the planet, the conviction that everything in the world is connected, the critique of new paradigms and forms of power derived from technology, the call to seek other ways of understanding the economy and progress, the value proper to each creature, the human meaning of ecology, the need for forthright and honest debate, the serious responsibility of international and local policy, the throwaway culture and the proposal of a new lifestyle (LS 16).

5. *The sense of mystery*

The third trajectory we can find in Pope Francis' magisterium under the heading of 'new relationships' brought about by Christ, is perhaps its underlying counterpoint and rhythm. In this case too he is speaking from personal experience of 'new relationships' there where, because of the in-breaking of the new world that emanates from the

---

6 This expression comes from R PESCH, *Von der 'Praxis des Himmels'. Kritische Elemente im Neuen Testament,* Styria, Graz-Wien-Köln 1972; It. tr. *Cristianesimo critico e prassi dell'amore alla luce del Nuovo Testamento,* Morcelliana, Brescia 1972.

resurrection of the Son made flesh in the Spirit, they are immersed in the Mystery that surrounds the trinitarian relationships of God in God and of God with us, and us in God. It is from there, God as Trinity, that everything begins, has its life, is accepted, redeemed and transfigured.

The 'sense of mystery', for Pope Francis, is 'trust in the invisible' that was made visible in Jesus and has been made available to us. 'It is true that this trust in the unseen can cause us to feel disoriented: it is like being plunged into the deep and not knowing what we will find. I myself have frequently experienced this' he tells us (*EG* 280). When I read these words, what immediately came to mind was what the Pope confided – only this once and unexpectedly, as I am led to believe – in an interview granted an intellectual engaged in painstaking research, Eugenio Scalfari, founder of the *La Repubblica* regarding his experience at being elected Pope:

> Before I accepted I asked if I could spend a few minutes in the room next to the one with the balcony overlooking the square. My head was completely empty and I was seized by a great anxiety. To make it go way and relax I closed my eyes and made every thought disappear, even the thought of refusing to accept the position, as the liturgical procedure allows. I closed my eyes and I no longer had any anxiety or emotion. At a certain point I was filled with a great light. It lasted a moment, but to me it seemed very long. Then the light faded, I got up suddenly and

walked into the room where the cardinals were waiting and the table on which was the act of acceptance. I signed it, the Cardinal Camerlengo countersigned it and then on the balcony there was the "Habemus Papam".[7]

The 'sense of mystery', For Pope Francis, is to dwell in the world knowing that we are always accepted in the depths of love and mercy which is God, so that we are then sent out to our brothers and sisters. It is to learn from Jesus how 'to rest in the tenderness of the arms of the Father amid our creative and generous commitment' (EG 279). It is 'allowing oneself to be guided by the Holy Spirit, renouncing the attempt to plan and control everything to the last detail, and instead letting him enlighten, guide and direct us, leading us wherever he wills. The Holy Spirit knows well what is needed in every time and place' (no. 280).

Immersion in Jesus in his relationship of love with his *Abba* due to the breath of life, freedom and communion which is the Spirit. Prayer, therefore, which in Jesus's prayer does not 'leave others out', with their flesh and their cross. If it did, it would be a hoax (cf. *EG* 281). Prayer 'full of people', prayer of intercession and thanksgiving for others (cf. nos 281-283). Prayer that is relationship and communion: 'a "leaven" in the heart of the Trinity. It is a way of penetrating the Father's heart and discovering new dimensions which can shed light on concrete situations and change them' (no. 283).

---

7   Interview published in "*La Reppublica*", 1 October 2013.

This form of prayer recalls the intensity and intentionality of the 'mental prayer' taught by Teresa of Avila and John of the Cross. In the wake of the teaching of Ignatius Loyola and Vatican II, it has established itself as the basis of a new way of thinking and acting beyond calculating and instrumental reason.

6. Having the same mind as Jesus and acting as Jesus would

This metamorphosis of *ratio* offered by *oratio* and drawn from *adoratio* as an 'emptying of self' in listening to oneself and welcoming the other, becomes the figure of an exercise in thinking by Pope Francis, starting from his dwelling in the place where the mysticism of 'flight of the alone to the alone'[8] intertwines with the mystique of 'As you, Father, are in me and I am in you, may they also be in us' (Jn 17:21).

The apophasis of silence blooms in the pericoresis [divine 'dance' of persons in the Trinity] *of 'body to body'* (cf. *EG* 88) *communication in the Spirit*. It is the 'sense of mystery' which ultimately dwells in and unceasingly leavens history:

> It involves knowing with certitude that all those who entrust themselves to God in love will bear good fruit (cf. Jn 15:5). This fruitfulness is often invisible, elusive and unquantifiable. We can know quite well that our lives will be fruitful, without claiming to know how, or where, or when. We may be sure that none of our acts of love will be lost, nor any of our acts of sincere concern for others. No single act of

---

8 PLOTINUS, *The Enneads*, VI, 9, 11.

> love for God will be lost, no generous effort is meaningless, no painful endurance is wasted. All of these encircle our world like a vital force ... The Holy Spirit works as he wills, when he wills and where he wills; we entrust ourselves without pretending to see striking results. We know only that our commitment is necessary (*EG* 279).

The inner dynamic of the gift – to God and others – since it is an exodus from self, an expropriation of self, an emptying of self which is open to being filled, a *kénosis* which opens up to *plérosis*.

As we read in Philippians 2:7, and too rarely do we insist on this, the *kénosis* of obedience in love is presented by Paul as a form of the 'new relationships brought by Jesus Christ.'[9] The Apostle explains that it is in him that the Philippians are constituted as a community: 'Let the same mind be in you that was in Christ Jesus.' The *phrónesis* (way of feeling, thinking and acting, practical wisdom) in force among them needs to be what they have received in Christ, and describes the personal and social dimension of having become, in him, a 'new creation'. They inform and affect one another, so much so that there cannot be one without the other.

This *phrónesis* is the same as Jesus has: subsisting in the form of God he 'empties himself' by receiving from the Father the Name which is above every other name. The Name which – as the Fourth Gospel teaches – the Son who

---

9 Cf. S Noceti, «*Abbiate in voi gli stessi sentimenti di Cristo» (Fil 2:5-11)*, in Aa. Vv, *Chiesa in Italia*. Annale 2014, Supplement to «Il regno» no. 11 on 15/12/2015, pp. 17-21.

became flesh (cf. Jn 1:14) received from the Father and the name by which he keeps the disciples 'one as we are one' (cf. Jn 17:11).

CHAPTER 5
FOUR WORDS TO REFORM THE CHURCH

1. *The Church, a people at the service of the coming of the Kingdom of God*

Thus far with Pope Francis we have been speaking about God and humanity and obviously have done so by looking at Jesus Christ today. It is thus that the Gospel of Jesus and the patrimony of the Christian tradition are alive and relevant in the experience and intelligence of Pope Francis' faith. Let us now briefly speak of his theological view of the Church in the wake of Vatican II.

The first thing to say is that for Pope Francis, now more than fifty years after the Council, 'the Church feels the need to keep this event alive.'[1] With it and because of it, we have been shifted forward, in fact been driven by the Spirit to a new phase of the two-thousand-year journey of which Vatican II marks a new and providential stage.

Paul VI even said it was as important as the Council of Nicaea, while others – I am thinking of a master of Italian theology like Luigi Sartori – have gone even further back to the so-called Council of Jerusalem. This means that in Vatican II as at Nicaea and Jerusalem, what is at stake

1 Pope Francis, *Misericordiae Vultus* (*MV*), 11 April 2017, no. 4.

(and how could it be anything other than this?) is once again the identity and mission of the event which is Jesus Christ, through his Church, in today's world: the unfolding in the here and now of the universal plan of God's love for humankind and creation which finds its living and eschatologically decisive centre in the Lord Jesus.

As we have already said, Pope Francis is the first pope not to have taken part in Vatican II, and he does not look back: nor does he take its reception in the Church's consciousness for granted. Seen this way the Council is a point of arrival, for sure, for an entire journey of renewal of the Church, but in the first instance it is a departure point and a launching pad for moving forward because the Holy Spirit is still urging it on, and humanity still cries out, tortured by its innumerable and excruciating wounds.

Therefore, the challenge that Pope Francis throws out to the Church, because the heart and mind *of God* is burning within him, is to stop any hesitation and start the exodus. On the other hand, it is enough to read Pope Paul VI's *Ecclesiam Suam* to hear the same urgency or to go back to John Paul II's *Duc in Altum* at the dawn of the third millennium.[2] Everything, in some way, is virtually contained in the clear and stringent description of the mystery of the Church that we find in the opening paragraph of *Lumen Gentium* (*LG*): 'the Church is in Christ like a sacrament or as a sign and instrument both of a very closely knit union with God and of the unity of the whole human race.'

---

2 Cf. Pope John Paul II, *Novo Millennio Ineunte*, 6 January 2001, no. 1.

This description invites us to look at the Church's mission with Jesus' eyes in order to conform the Church to him. It is not a question of the Church as a *societas perfecta* drawing its parameters for understanding and action from a historical individual in society who has been defined once and for all, nor is it simply a question of the relationship between spiritual and temporal power seen from the point of view of Christianity through history. It is looking at the Church from the point of view of the coming of the Kingdom of God among human beings as a people called to distribute the yeast and salt which makes the life that does not die present in history, the life that comes from God alone and can only be fulfilled in God.

Everything in the Church is at the service of this: the Word proclaimed, the Sacraments celebrated, the 'hierarchical gifts', 'charismatic gifts', the social, cultural and political involvement of the lay faithful. It is about being a 'sign', in every expression of the life and mission of the Church from the smallest to the most universal, of perceptible and credible experiences of union with God and unity among brothers and sisters. It is about becoming an effective 'instrument', with an action of proclamation and testimony that is both consistent and fascinating – an effective tool that rises from the inside and gives the taste of life that does not die to the life of the world.

The Church is the people, then, 'the initial budding forth of the Kingdom' (cf. *LG* 5). This people looks to Christ, relives Christ in the light and strength of the Spirit. It exists and works not for itself but for others. It holds onto and nourishes the desire for new a heaven and a new earth as the breath of life and hope in its commitment to building freedom, justice and fraternity among individuals and peoples.

This is today's world: terrorism, persecutions, social injustice, war, hunger, mass migration of biblical proportions as we see today, the dictatorship of today's technocratic ideology and profit, the environmental crisis … they all besmirch the face of the human family and our common home to the extent that our very existence is threatened.

It is not difficult to understand how it is that the 'idea' of the Church and its mission according to the heart of Jesus which Vatican II focused on, is now pulsing through the thoughts and feelings, the very veins, I would say, of Pope Francis. *According to the heart of Jesus.* It has not always been something taken for granted, nor can it be taken for granted even now, that the Church is meant to express the form and style of Jesus. There always has been and still is the subtle temptation to think of the Church as the herald of the gospel, yes, but as a human institution necessarily forced to come to some sort of agreement with the world's logic (at the political, economic, cultural level). While the gospel knows no compromise, the Church – one ends up thinking, unfortunately – is forced to at least yield in some areas: and not just out of human weakness but due to the very necessity of it all, due to *Realpolitik*, to keep its feet on the ground.

The implication of this is that we need to take a clear look at the evidence and courageously develop some directions for renewal that the Holy Spirit has shown the Church through the Council. Gradually, over the decades and through some highs and lows, these have been becoming clearer in the Church's self-understanding through the magisterium of the Popes and Episcopal Conferences and are at work deep within the journey of the people of God in the various contexts of its life.

Pope Francis is gathering them up and putting them before our eyes: his prophetic determination, persuasive communication, pastoral incisiveness present them as essential paths to be followed to the end, faithful to the gospel and the Church's teaching, combined with the creativity that comes from obedience to the urging of the Holy Spirit and listening to the challenging signs of our times. I would sum all this up in four words which frequently appear in whatever Pope Francis says, and which throw light on his gestures in the demanding perspective of reforming the Church:[3] *mercy, synodality, poverty, encounter.*

2. *'The medicine of mercy'*

The first key word to illuminate the ministry of Pope Francis is the primacy of the 'medicine of mercy', to use the terms John XXIII used when describing the tone he wanted for Vatican II and the new season the Church has been called to in its mission. Pope Francis says that 'It is a process going on for years in the Church. It is clear that the Lord

---

3 On the significance and implications of this priority in Pope Francis' ministry, cf. A SPADARO – CM GALLI (Eds.), *La riforma e le riforme nella Chiesa,* Queriniana, Brescia 2016.

asked for a renewal in the Church of this attitude of mercy.'[4]

Drawing from the mystery of God the Father who reveals himself in Christ and in the ceaseless activity of the Holy Spirit in the history of the world. Mercy both describes and aims at the realism, impact and prophecy of the Christian vision of things. It expresses the vital, effective perception that the truth of the gospel is God's love for human beings as they are and not as they should be according to some abstract theory. This love then accompanies them in becoming what they are called to become in God's plan, according to the wise law of gradualness: welcomed healed, accompanied and encouraged by the love of the Father who is 'rich in mercy' (Eph 2:4), by the Son who became flesh and died on the cross for us, and by the Holy Spirit who has been abundantly poured into our hearts where he utters an inward call for us to be adopted as sons and daughters.

Mercy is the prism through which to see and testify to the joyful and liberating truth and transforming power of the gospel. It does not mean putting truth and justice in parentheses. Far from it! It means focusing on and communicating what is at its core: love. As Fr Raniero Cantalamessa says: 'Mercy is not a surrogate for truth and justice, but is a condition for being able to find these. It is not an indication of weakness but of strength.'[5] At the right moment it demands that the beauty and fullness of truth be

---

[4] POPE FRANCIS, *Dialogue with the Polish Bishops* (Krakow, 27 July 2016), 02-08-2016).

[5] R CANTALAMESSA, *Il valore politico della misericordia*, in *L'Osservatore Romano*, 30 March 2008.

manifested, when it can be accepted, desired and achieved, even in its dizzying heights. This is always and only possible through the grace of God at work in the heart of every human being. Did not St Augustine write that until it has been understood that the meaning of every truth and commandment expressed by the Holy Scriptures is charity, we are still far from understanding the truth?[6]

The primacy of mercy as lifestyle and mission, which Pope Francis is proposing is first of all a crucible of purification for the life of the Church and discernment of its presence in history. The Church is reborn daily, made spotless by the waters of baptism and the sacrifice of the Eucharist which generates social interaction. It extends and passes on this experience of grace, in which it is always recreated by the Spirit of the Risen Lord, in the myriad of forms of its being and activity in love at the service of humankind: from forgiveness of sins to looking after those who suffer and are marginalized, from its commitment to justice to its fostering the common good, to its intellectual charity of thought and culture.

Here, we can see, is the real key to the Apostolic Exhortation *Amoris Laetitia* (*AL*). It is not about making concessions with regard to the truth of the call to evangelical perfection, but of becoming one with each person and from

---

6 Cf. AUGUSTINE, *De Doctrina Christiana*, I, 36.40: "Whoever, then, thinks that he understands the Holy Scriptures, or any part of them, but puts such an interpretation upon them as does not tend to build up this twofold love of God and our neighbour, does not yet understand them as he ought" (http://www.newadvent.org/fathers/12021.htm).

within each situation lovingly disclosing the way that leads to God, as the Apostle Paul did: 'To the weak I became weak, so that I might win the weak. I have become all things to all people, that I might by all means save some' (1 Cor 9:22).[7]

> Using an image that at first can catch us off-guard, Pope Francis speaks of the Church as a 'field hospital'. It is a metaphor which translates Jesus' approach in the parable of the Good Samaritan, which Paul VI made his own to express what he wanted the Church, with Vatican II, to be and do. Here are his words: 'The old story of the Samaritan has been the model of the spirituality of the council ... Errors were condemned, indeed, because charity demanded this no less than did truth, but for the persons themselves there was only warning, respect and love. Instead of depressing diagnoses, encouraging remedies; instead of direful prognostics, messages of trust ... all this rich teaching is channelled in one direction, the service of mankind, of every condition, in every weakness and need'[8]

Faced with the immense tragedies and enormous

---

7 Cf. POPE FRANCIS, *Address to representatives at the 5th National Congress of the Italian Church*, Florence, 10 November 2015.

8 POPE PAUL VI, *Address during the last general meeting of the Second Vatican Council*, 7 December 1965; mentioned by Pope Francis in the Bull of Indiction of the Extraordinary Jubilee of Mercy, MV, no. 4.

problems afflicting humanity today, perhaps this image of the 'field hospital' is an eloquent one for the Church's motherly heart to be using – this Church which is the sign and instrument, in Jesus, of union with God in doing his will and in being close to its brothers and sisters. The injuries to be treated in this hospital are not just physical ones but also the ones that affect the heart, the soul, the spirit, intelligence, will. To speak of a 'field hospital' makes us understand the seriousness of the situation humanity is in, torn by an ideological war where the very truth and beauty of God's image in humankind is at stake, these human beings created as male and female to reflect the fruitful life of communion of the Blessed Trinity.

'Field hospital', yes, using the strongest medicine, mercy, as testimony to the truth of love, to tackle one of the most serious risks humankind has run since we began, the risk of overturning God the Creator's plan for his creation, as Pope Francis said to the Polish Bishops quoting Pope Benedict.[9]

And this is even without saying what mercy – internalized in our mind and heart and taken as a criterion of judgement and action – has to become by impacting with realism and vision on politics, economy and law. Where this occurs, it changes the face of the earth. In the political scene, for example, mercy leads to never thinking that a situation or individual is lost forever, but is about being open to the glimmer of change just barely visible in every situation, and to the flexibility that might come from unforeseeable

---

9 Pope Benedict's words as quoted by Pope Francis: "This is the age of sin against God the Creator!"

solutions with a view to facing up to conflicts in order to transform them into links in a chain of a new process (cf. *EG* 227). And this, to the point of the dizzying and scandalous evangelical openness to the most effective force of all, because in it, through Christ's cross, the newness of his Resurrection acts: the newness of forgiveness and love for our enemies (cf. Lk 6:27).

3. Synodality: what God expects of his Church

'Church and Synod are synonymous', Pope Francis emphasized, quoting John Chrysostom, in his address at the ceremony commemorating the 50th anniversary of the institution of the Synod of Bishops, going on to explain: 'It is precisely this path of synodality which God expects of the Church of the third millennium.' In concrete terms this means that in the Church, 'as in an inverted pyramid, the top is located beneath the base'; that 'the only authority' is the authority of Jesus which is 'the authority of service'; that a synodal Church is a Church which listens: 'to listen to God, so that with him we may hear the cry of his people; to listen to his people until we are in harmony with the will to which God calls us.'[10]

This is one of the demanding and delicate issues which the International Theological Commission is currently working on. It is a question of imagining and treading the right paths for embodying the ecclesiology of the people of

---

10 POPE FRANCIS, *Address at the ceremony commemorating the 50th anniversary of the institution of the Synod of Bishops*, 17 October 2015.

God and communion we find in Vatican II, and in fidelity to the tradition, in institutional ways as well. There is no need to go immediately or only to the canonical issues and procedural matters of diocesan and provincial and bishops synods. Rather is there a need to to look at synodality as a pervasive and ongoing spirit and style of being Church in which the disciples of Jesus journey together – which is what 'synod' actually means: from the Greek *sýn* = with, and *hodós* = road – among people to testify to the newness, beauty and power of the coming of the Kingdom of God.

A priority in the awareness and involvement of the entire Church is at stake here: beginning with the bishops, who must be the ones whop set the process in motion and guide it. Otherwise the subject of this new stage of evangelization we are called to will not take off. And this subject is the entire people of God in its variety and unity, in and through which the risen Jesus manifests and exercises his *exousía*, his power and sway for salvation of humanity. The specific and essential apostolic authority which the Pastors have is given and used in service of the manifestation of this *exousía* of the Risen Lord who makes his presence felt in the Church in many ways: in the *sensus fidei* of the faithful, in the charismatic gifts that enlivens them, in the competence the laity have in temporal matters … The authority of the Pastors is one of promoting, sifting, guiding, giving direction to the *exousía* of the Risen Lord in his variegated yet convergent manifestation through the inalienable contribution of all the members and states of life in the people of God.

It is a matter of putting all the gifts that everyone has into circulation, be they big or small, and for everyone to have the possibility of speaking up boldly and humbly, speaking charitably with one another and under the guidance of their Pastors, in communion with them and with the Successor of Peter, knowing how to discern together what the Spirit is saying to the Church today; to every local Church, Churches in the same region, the universal Church.

This is what synodality is. It is a process of reform – and before that, of spiritual conversion – which demands time, patience, formation, everyone's involvement. Suffice it to think of the kind of bishop and priest needed to set this motion in process and keep it going: this kind of bishop doesn't just come from nowhere, nor does the competent priest with evangelical wisdom, capacity for discernment, someone who governs authoritatively and is the living soul and sure guide of this exodus from one way of thinking and building up the Church to another more compliant with the vocation of the people of God. And then to do it in communion with his brothers in the episcopate and the presbyterate and with all the people of God. A similar discourse applies to consecrated life, movements, new communities, the laity, women …

Really, there is so much to do, as Pope Francis remarked, perhaps with a deliberate intention to provoke, in his Letter to Cardinal Marc Ouellet, President of the Pontifical Commission for Latin America: 'I remember the famous phrase "it is the hour of the laity", but it seems the clock has stopped!'[11]

Of course it is difficult, even risky, to go in this direction. But we need to trust in God and in the gifts he spreads so abundantly among the people of God. If the time has come for synodality, as the Pope Francis says, it means that the ground is ready. We need to have courage and prudence, serenity and decision, foresight and vigilance.

4. *'A poor Church for the poor'*

Here is the third item that stands out in the magisterium and testimony of Pope Francis. It is not about being paupers but about the truth of the gospel, the *forma Ecclesiae* from which the *forma Christi* must shine out ever more brightly and luminously. The option for the poor, as John Paul II teaches us, is 'a special form of primacy in the exercise of Christian charity, to which the whole tradition of the Church bears witness'[12] This option, as Benedict XVI emphasized, is 'implicit in the Christological faith in the God who became poor for us, so as to enrich us with his poverty.'[13]

There is a further sign and message which came to us at the moment Jorge Mario Bergoglio was elected to the Chair of Peter, when he felt in his heart that he was called

---

11 POPE FRANCIS, Letter to Cardinal Marc Ouellet, President of the Pontifical Commission for Latin America, 19 March 2016.

12 POPE JOHN PAUL II, Encyclical *Sollicitudo Rei Socialis*, 30 December 1987, no. 42.

13 POPE BENEDICT XVI, *Address to the opening session of the 5th General Conference of the Latin American and Caribbean Episcopate*, Aparecida, 13 May 2007.

to take on the name Francis. The Council had spoken of 'the poor Church for the poor' and in vibrant words, but in the end they seemed to be marginal ones.[14] Paul VI, in *Ecclesiam Suam*, had sought to strongly emphasize poverty alongside charity as the specific quality of the Church in our times.[15] Following the difficult and challenging period of liberation theology but before and quite decidedly beginning with the experience of suffering and sharing the Church in Latin America had been through (and not only this Church), it is no coincidence that we get this clear and lofty message fifty years after the Council, from the first pope to come 'from the end of the world'.

What kind of poverty are we talking about? The poverty of a 'poor' Church 'for the poor'. The poverty of the Church that experiences the 'greatest poverty' of heart, mind and means which conform it to, and I would say crucify it on the same cross its Lord was crucified on: because it is from him, through the Church, that the richness of God's grace can flow out upon the world. It is the poverty which is gift of self, love; the poverty experienced in the life of communion of the Blessed Trinity where, as Jesus says, '*omnia mea tua sunt – all that is mine is yours*' (cf. Lk 15:31) and from where the glory of the crucified God shines out.

But it is not only a question of a Church that lives by and in this poverty. It is a question of a Church that wants

14 Cf. for example, regarding the contribution of Cardinal Giacomo Lecaro in inserting this theme in the drawing up of *LG*, no. 8; cf. M Donati, *Il sogno di una Chiesa. Gli interventi al Concilio Vaticano II del Card. G. Lercaro*, Cittadella, Assisi 2010.

15 Cf. *Ecclesiam Suam*, nos 55-56.

to and becomes a Church of the poor, breaking free from all idolatrous security of human power and wealth. A Church that lives with, for, and in those people where the stigma of poverty – be it material, moral, spiritual – plagues the flesh, face and heart of humanity. This is Christ's place. This is the Church's place, since it is with and for all people and hence must be with the poor. In this regard too, conversion and reform which begin with the heart involve the lifestyle, structures, aspirations, judgement criteria and programs of the Church on mission.

5. *The prophecy of the 'culture of encounter'*

Finally, following in the footsteps of Paul VI's *Ecclesiam Suam*, Pope Francis often speaks of dialogue as the crucial way of proclaiming the gospel. Addressing bishops in the United States, he encouraged them as follows:

> Dialogue is our method, not as a shrewd strategy but out of fidelity to the One who never wearies of visiting the marketplace, even at the eleventh hour, to propose his offer of love (Mt 20:1-16) ... Do not be afraid to set out on that "exodus" which is necessary for all authentic dialogue. Otherwise, we fail to understand the thinking of others, or to realize deep down that the brother or sister we wish to reach and redeem, with the power and the closeness of love, counts more than their positions, distant as they may be from what we hold as true and certain.[16]

16 Washington D.C., 23 September 2015.

These words are clear about the conversion of heart, mind and style asked of us and which, furthermore, comes as a coherent and persuasive whole from adopting the synodal style and attitude of mercy which describe the Church's mission.

But Francis also often uses another phrase, one that may even be richer, more emphatic and concrete: 'Encounter, the culture of encounter.' Encounter says that we need to deal with each other through dialogue, deal with difference, and that means leaving our difference behind in order to encounter, accept, discover the other so we can walk together with him or her and do something that is just and beautiful together. And do so with expectation, desire, joy, even if we need to see that from the beginning of our encounter with the other our sense of security, our established points of view and customs may well be at risk. Yet, in a process of mutual enrichment we end up surprising ourselves, the other too, in that surprise of all surprises which is God's love for all his sons and daughters. Antonio Rosmini has a very eloquent neologism for expressing this ethical imperative which translates the vocation of the human individual: *inaltrarsi*, or a form of mutual intersubjectivity, going out to each other.

Christianity, ultimately, is the religion which states inclusively (by contemplating God who is One and Three and Creator): 'It is good that the other exists.'[17] The Father and the Son, Creator and creature, man and woman, all

---

17 This expression comes from H.U. von Balthasar in his *Teo-drammatica*, V, It tr. Jaca Book, Milan, 1996, p. 70. The work exists in English as *Theo-Drama: Theological Dramatic Theory: The Last Act* (Vol 5) Ignatius Press April 1998.

the different peoples. Cultures and traditions. Otherness and diversity, understood properly, are not the principle of what is relative but of what is relational, not the principle of anarchy but of harmony in the richness and joy of the Holy Spirit. Is there not here, as well, a key for reforming the outlook and activity of the Church and making it more compliant with the outlook and activity of Jesus?

Pope Francis cuts through everything with a simple, clear example: we either build bridges or we build walls! *Tertium non datur*. There is no alternative. This is the psychologically and spiritually evident practical principle of Christian anthropology and sociology which are, by definition, essentially and prophetically trinitarian. Nor is it necessary to underline how revolutionary this principle is – from the religious but also cultural, social, political and economic point of view – for the decisive contribution that the Church is called to offer, in the wake of *Gaudium et Spes*, and the Church's social doctrine from Paul VI's *Populorum Progressio* on to Benedict XVI's *Caritas in Veritate*, and finally Francis' *Laudato Si'*, all aiming to determine guidelines for the change of cultural paradigm all of humanity today is involved in, without any possibility of going back. It is a paradigm that needs to affect our way of imagining and managing social, political, economic relationships from a perspective that starts from the poor, the marginalized, the discarded, the geographical and existential peripheries, and guide and shape technical and scientific development according to a logic that is determined by caring for our common home.

And let us not forget that the crucial question today for being able to do all this is, as we have emphasized, 'rethinking thinking'. The culture of Christian inspiration and the pedagogical talent that inspire the Church cannot remain on the sidelines or simply be tossed into this crucial undertaking, Pope Francis exhorts us. There is a need for resolute faith in the gospel's unparalleled human potential, for an extraordinary legacy of thinking and action to be taken up responsibly, for clarity of vision and the courage, led by the Holy Spirit, to responsibly undertake new ways which respond to the *kairós* of God in our times.

***

Mercy, synodality, poverty, encounter. There are other words in the message that the Spirit addresses to us today which can give impetus to spiritual and pastoral reform and conversion. But without a doubt, these words invite us, with the enlightened understanding of the faith, to an examination of conscience and a leap in quality. 'The reform of the Church ... is not exhausted in the countless plans to change her structures. It instead means being implanted and rooted in Christ, allowing herself to be led by the Spirit. Thus everything will be possible with genius and creativity.'[18]

---

18   Pope Francis, *Address to representatives at the 5th National Congress of the Italian Church*, cit.

www.ingramcontent.com/pod-product-compliance
Lightning Source LLC
Chambersburg PA
CBHW051952290426
44110CB00015B/2207